Published by Possibilities Publishing
22 Amherst Road
Amherst, MA 01002
413-253-3488
1-800-822-2801
413-253-3490 (fax)
www.possibilitiespublisher.com

ISBN 0-87425-596-1

Editorial services by Mary George
Production services by Jean Miller
Cover design by Donna Thibault-Wong

The Possibilities Leader- The New Science of Possibilities Managemen

by

Robert R. Carkhuff, Ph.D.
and
Bernard G. Berenson, Ph.D.

Contributor:
Christopher J. Carkhuff, M.A. Cert.

This book is dedicated to John T. Kelly, Manager, IBM's Office of the Future, who conducted the first private-sector research on the interdependent organizational relationships of Human, Information, and Organizational Capital Development.

The Possibilities Leader—
The New Science of Possibilities Management

CONTENTS

About the Authors ix
About the Contributor xi
Foreword *by Barry Cohen, Ph.D.* xiii
Preface xix
Welcome to a Special Kind of Book! xxv

I. INTRODUCTION AND OVERVIEW **1**
1. Possibilities Management—The Processing Paradigm **3**
Probabilities and Possibilities 10
Possibilities Management Paradigm 15
Interdependent Processing Systems 15
Organizational Management Functions 18

II. THE I^5 POSSIBILITIES MANAGEMENT SYSTEMS **23**
2. I^1—Information Relating Systems **25**
Case: The Possibilities Leader—I^1 Information Relating 29
Information Relating Systems 32
Relating: An Introduction 34
Conceptual Information 35
Relating to Conceptual Information 36
Operational Information 38
Relating to Operational Information 39
Information Relating Skills 41
Relating-Skills Training 46
Attending 47
Responding to Concepts 49
Responding to Operations 51
Personalizing Operations 52
Initiating Operations 54
Summary and Transition 55
Case: The Possibilities Leader (continued) 57

3. ***I^2—Information Representing Systems*** **59**
Case: The Possibilities Leader—I^2 Information Representing 63
Information Representing Systems 70
Relating to Operational Phenomena 72
The Image Maker 77
Information Representing Skills 78
One-Dimensional Information 80
Two-Dimensional Information 82
Three-Dimensional Information 83
"Nested"-Dimensional Information 85
Multidimensional Information 87
The Information Modeler 90
In Transition 97
Case: The Possibilities Leader (continued) 99

4. ***I^3—Individual Processing Systems*** **101**
Case: The Possibilities Leader—I^3 Individual Processing 105
Individual Processing Systems 109
The Discriminative Learners 111
Individual Processing Skills 114
Goaling 115
Analyzing 117
Synthesizing 118
Operationalizing 119
Technologizing 121
The Generative Thinker 123
In Transition 130
Case: The Possibilities Leader (continued) 131

5. ***I^4—Interpersonal Processing Systems*** **133**
Case: The Possibilities Leader—I^4 Interpersonal Processing 137
Interpersonal Processing Systems 141
The Situational Manager 143
Interpersonal Processing Skills 145
Goaling 145
Getting 146
Giving 147

Growing 147
Going 148
The Interpersonal Manager 150
In Transition 151
Case: The Possibilities Leader (continued) 153

6. *I^5—Interdependent Processing Systems* **155**
Case: The Possibilities Leader—I^5 Interdependent Processing 159
Interdependent Processing Systems 164
The Planning Leader 166
Inductive Generating 175
Deductive Innovation 178
MCD 179
OCD 180
HCD 181
ICD 183
mCD 184
The Processing Leader 187
In Transition 196
Case: The Possibilities Leader (concluded) 197

III. SUMMARY AND TRANSITION **203**
7. *Process-Centric Change* **205**
The Processing Team 211
The Possibilities Management Paradigm 220

Selected Publications by Authors 229
Acknowledgments 231

About the Authors

Dr. Robert R. Carkhuff is Founder and Chairperson, The Carkhuff Group: Human Technology, Inc., Human Resource Development Press, Inc., and Carkhuff Thinking Systems, Inc. One of the most frequently referenced writers in the social sciences, Dr. Carkhuff has authored many major works, including ***Human Processing & Human Productivity, Sources of Human Productivity, The Exemplar, Empowering,*** and ***The Age of the New Capitalism.***

Dr. Bernard G. Berenson is Executive Director, Carkhuff Institute of Applied Science and Human Technology. A professor at the state universities of Maryland, Massachusetts, and New York, Dr. Berenson was co-founder of the original Center for Human Resource Development and chairperson of its graduate training program at American International College. He is the author of ***Sources of Growth in Counseling and Psychotherapy*** and ***Beyond Counseling and Therapy,*** as well as contributing author to ***The Development of Human Resources, Helping and Human Relations,*** and many other books.

Together, Carkhuff and Berenson have introduced several market revolutions over the past four decades. They brought us the first interpersonal skills system in the '60s and '70s. They introduced the first individual models of human resource development in the '70s and '80s. Their combined efforts also initiated us into twenty-first-century thinking *in the '80s* with the first models of new leadership and organizational capital development. Now, as creators of ***The New Science of Possibilities,*** Carkhuff and Berenson are the first scientists to address the area of management.

About the Contributor

CHRISTOPHER CARKHUFF is Director, Research and Development, Carkhuff Thinking Systems, Inc., and contributor to Chapter 6, I^5—Interdependent Processing Systems.

Foreword

by Barry Cohen, Ph.D.
Vice President, Marketing
Parametric Technology Corporation

In ***The Possibilities Organization,*** Carkhuff and Berenson entered the phenomenal experience of the organization. They merged with the organization to become *"one"* with it; they generated entirely new images of organizational possibilities; they innovated within these images to deliver to us the first systematic approach to birthing and growing organizations with infinite possibilities.

Now, in ***The Possibilities Leader,*** Carkhuff and Berenson introduce us to how they process to generate organizational possibilities. They teach us how to process interdependently to generate new and powerful images of any phenomena—people, data, or things. They also teach us how to process interdependently to innovate within the phenomena and initiate totally new phenomenal operations. In so doing, they teach us a whole new language of processing. People will never be the same!

The Possibilities Leader is a book about a *"paradigm shift"* in management from probabilities science to possibilities science—although, in truth, current management practices hardly qualify as a paradigm, let alone a science! *Scientific management,* the platform upon which twentieth-century probabilities management was based, is no more than a euphemism for totalitarian rule: command and control policy, classist organizations, conditioned personnel, and the rest. *Possibilities management,* then, is more than a paradigm shift: it is the first authentic management paradigm, the first model that actually defines all of the processing systems required by the twenty-first-century manager, and all of the new capital development functions to which those systems are dedicated.

First, let us take a brief look at the processing systems:

I^1 Information relating systems to define phenomenal operations;

I^2 Information representing systems to dimensionalize images of phenomena;

I^3 Individual processing systems to generate new images of phenomena;

I^4 Interpersonal processing systems to generate more powerful images of phenomena;

I^5 Interdependent processing systems to generate the most powerful images of phenomena.

Interdependently and synergistically related, these processing systems define the core of the manager's contribution to any phenomena, especially *tasks-in-mind.*

Next, let us view the organizational functions to which the processing is dedicated. They are labeled "new capital development systems" to represent their contributions in the equation for generating wealth. There are five functions in all:

MCD Marketplace capital development, or continuous marketplace positioning;

OCD Organizational capital development, or continuous organizational alignment;

HCD Human capital development, or continuous human processing;

ICD Information capital development, or continuous information modeling;

mCD Mechanical capital development, or continuous mechanical tooling.

When the interdependent processing systems are dedicated to organizational functions, they generate new capital development. For the first time in the history of business, managers know what they are doing and where they are going. We have a real paradigm to guide us!

But this book does more than simply present a paradigm. It builds a bridge that spans not only probabilities and possibilities science, but also probabilities and possibilities *culture.* The authors empower us to actualize a culture of true freedom: genuine free-enterprise-driven economies, truly free and direct democratic governance, all empowered by free scientific processing systems—by, in a word, *"process-centricity."*

In a *process-centric* culture, everything is processing. There is no enduring content. One processor's outputs are another's inputs. All processors' interdependent processing is spiraling and changing, as are the phenomena that they process. In short, processing is an accelerator of evolution wherein we can continuously influence our continuously changing destinies.

In a process-centric culture, all models of processing are powerful and elegant. As the authors demonstrate, even the formula for generating wealth can be reduced to simple yet potent terms:

I^5 represents the interdependent processing systems of possibilities management. NCD represents the organization's new capital development systems, which generate wealth. I^5 and NCD are related interdependently and synergistically: each contributes to the other's growth. We managers may now become *process-centric* in a wealth-generating culture!

The possibilities leader is the source of the New Capitalism.

Preface

Sometime in the last decade of the twentieth century, civilization crossed a momentous threshold. It moved from shaping cultures based upon past traditions to generating cultures to meet future requirements. Because of spiraling changes in technology-driven economies, the historic traditions no longer sufficed. Ninety percent of the scientific and technological *"breakthroughs"* in the history of humankind occurred in that last decade, and now generate robust, new socioeconomic requirements that we must meet in order to participate in the marketplace. Our traditional responses, no matter how enduring, have been rendered impotent. The requirements that define our new century are *prepotent.*

Nowhere are these emerging requirements seen more clearly than in the economic arena. The traditional assumption of the twentieth-century marketplace was independence: the traditional function of that marketplace was competitiveness. They no longer work:

- Command and control economies are collapsing.
- Totalitarian governments are disappearing.
- Closed ideologies are cannibalizing themselves.
- Monolithic organizations are fragmenting.
- Authoritarian bosses are on extinction schedules.

Everyone, and everything, has discovered the emerging universal truth of change: no one, and nothing, knows everything! Independence and competition are now depressor variables in the equation for wealth generation.

What replaces these now-burdensome traditions is the emerging requirements of the twenty-first-century marketplace: interdependence and collaboration. Only interdependently concerned and collaboratively achieved initiatives can meet and exceed the spiraling socioeconomic challenges and, indeed, generate further challenges. Here we are speaking of the following necessities:

- Networked economies in the free-enterprise marketplace;
- Partnered private and public sectors within free democratic governance;
- Collaborative scientific study in free and open societies;

- Self-organizing, partnered *"possibilities organizations";*
- Interrelated and empowered people capable of generating all of the above.

To be sure, America has been the experiment for defining the interdependent and collaborative requirements for the twenty-first-century global marketplace. In science and technology alone, American or American-affiliated people and organizations have been responsible for 90 percent of the breakthroughs that drive our economy.

"Interdependency" is perhaps the most difficult of all words to define. That is because it has been alien to the human experience, which itself has been defined historically by our technologies and our activities:

- Fourteen million years of dependency as hunter-gatherers and basic tool-makers;
- Ten thousand years of searching for elusive, illusory independency as agrarian farmers, industrial workers, and information technologists.

It is only now—at the beginning of the twenty-first century—that interdependency has become a requirement for participation in the global marketplace.

In many ways, it is easier to define interdependency by what it is *not* than by what it is. *Interdependency is not mutual dependency.* Mutual dependency conveys an image of drowning swimmers with their arms around each other. We simply cannot ante up to the table of interdependency with dependency.

Now let us turn to what interdependency *is:*

> ***Interdependency is continuous and partnered phenomenal processing for mutual benefits.***

Phenomena are entities—people, data, things—with operational dimensions: functions, or outputs, derived from environmental conditions; components, or inputs, dedicated to discharging the functions; processes, or procedures, that enable the components to discharge the functions. Processing, in turn, is the thinking that generates new and changing images of phenomena. In this context, let us define the term *"interdependency":*

The functions are mutual growth benefits. The components are partnered (or mutual) phenomenal relationships. The processes are continuous phenomenal processing. Now we may define interdependency in operational terms:

> ***Mutual benefits are accomplished by partnered phenomena enabled by continuous phenomenal processing systems.***

In other words, we partner up with other phenomena to engage in continuous processing for mutual benefits.

Now let us analyze the ingredients of interdependency.

First of all, the components are phenomena that get together or partner for mutual purposes. The phenomena involve people, data, or things that relate to generate. Often such people, sophisticated in knowledge of the phenomena, represent the phenomena in *"virtual processing."*

Second, the processes that transform components into functions emphasize continuous phenomenal processing:

- Within, between, and among phenomena represented by *"virtual processors,"*
- Within, between, and among people and *"virtual"* phenomena, individually and/or interpersonally.

The phenomenal processing is continuous because the phenomena are continuously changing: if the phenomena change, the processing changes; if the processors change, the phenomena change.

Third, the functions are mutual growth benefits. Both the phenomena that are represented *"virtually"* and the processors will be beneficiaries of growth. Of course, the mutual processors can grow only to the level of their processing abilities. However, if they engage in continuous processing, they will grow synergistically within, between, and among the phenomena.

Interdependent processing, then, is the generative source of new capital development in an organization. Interdependent processing means fully entering the experience of the phenomena: the individual tasks to be performed; the teaming objectives to be achieved; the systems goals to be accomplished; the organizational architecture to be aligned; the corporate missions to be defined.

> How many of you can truly say that you are dedicated interdependent processors within the phenomenal experience of the organization?

Many people believe that they process interdependently at least some of the time, if not most of the time. Wrong! How can you process interdependently when you do not even know what interdependent processing is? Corporate executives might claim that they relate interdependently to their assignments, but the facts suggest otherwise. Documentation of tens of thousands of corporate meetings, telephone conversations, and other forms of communication indicate that less than 10 percent of executive time is free for thinking. And it is doubtful whether one percent of that time is used for thought, given other executive pursuits.

Fortunately for all of us, capitalism is truly a theory of change. The term "capital" simply means what is *"most important."* For ages, we equated capitalism with financial capital, defining it as the wherewithal to bring land, labor, and (later on) machinery together in a *"productive agency"*—what we now refer to as "the organization." But capitalism has evolved.

The new capitalism incorporates interdependent processing and capital ingredients in the equation for generating wealth. These ingredients emphasize five types of capital: marketplace, organizational, human, information, and mechanical. Financial capital is reduced to a catalyst that makes new capital development, or NCD, possible.

This evolved capitalism has four important features.

First, interdependent processing systems are dedicated to new capital development systems in organizations. Conversely, the new capital development systems are dedicated to interdependent processing systems: the acquisition, application, and transfer of interdependent phenomenal processing to generate and innovate new and powerful images of all phenomena.

Second, the new capitalism conceives of these NCD ingredients as processing systems. This does not mean capitalism has abandoned its planning systems, only that it seeks to drive them by processing systems. Without processing and possibilities thinking, probabilities planning is entropic: it increasingly cannibalizes its past planning efforts and, in doing so, discards its most valuable source of possibilities—the so-called *"error variance."* In short, the new capitalism is process-centric and possibilities-driven.

Third, the new capitalism is interdependent in nature. Precisely because capitalism is an open system, it incorporates the essential interdependency of nature and its human products. Precisely because the NCD ingredients are interdependently related, capitalism is interdependent with the synergistic, mutual-growth-generating functions of these ingredients.

Finally, capitalism *is* interdependent processing. *All* phenomenal systems are interdependent processing systems. Such systems generate the interdependent processing systems of NCD in organizations, and vice versa.

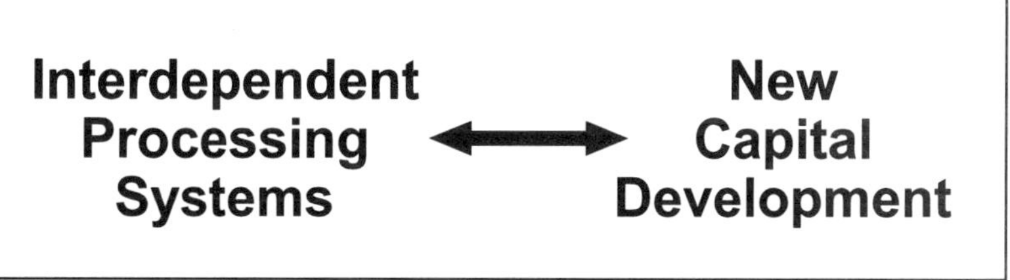

The possibilities leaders know this, believe this, and are skilled in the implementation of capitalism as a possibilities science. Interdependent processing is the source of the new capitalism.

Welcome To A Special Kind of Book!

This is a book of pictures. We call the pictures *information models.* Information models are the universal language of processing in the twenty-first century. They are the interdependent and synergistic processing partners with human processors or human capital. We relate to phenomena, represent them, and then generate increasingly more powerful information models of the phenomena. That is the thesis of this book: interdependent processing generates prepotent models of phenomena. The reader need not conquer the processing operations involved: there is time for that later with different experiences and materials. The reader need only experience the magical images of any and all phenomena; to be introduced to the generation of powerful possibilities; to realize the accomplishments of generations of work in an afternoon of processing.

RRC and BGB

The equation for wealth is an evolving one. As marketplace requirements change, the capital ingredients change. Conventional wisdom aside, "capital" simply means what is "most important." Superstitious behavior to the contrary, financial capital is no longer "most important." Today, finances account for less than 15 percent of the variance in economic productivity growth. The emerging ingredients of new capital development account for more than 85 percent of growth.

I

Introduction and Overview

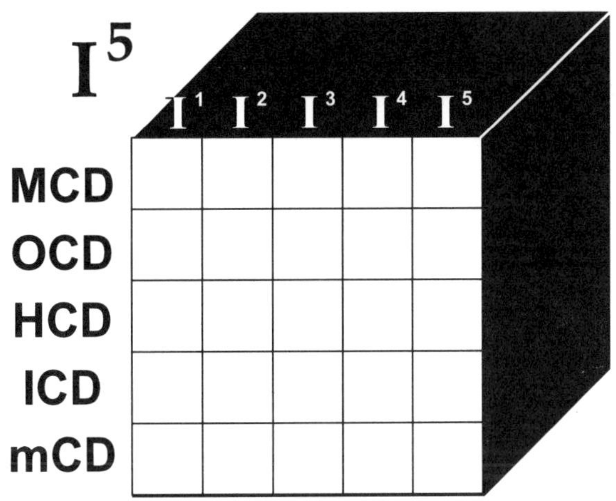

1 Possibilities Management—The Processing Paradigm

Process-centricity is the generative source of wealth.

"Oh, my God!" Franklin Taylor exclaimed. "The bridge is out. We have gone a bridge too far." He eyed the slothful peasants lingering around the rising river. He and his family were at their mercy. He feared their motives. Then he shifted into aristocratic gear: "Better to be safe than sorry!" He put to use the one principle he had derived from his privileged educational background: "They [the peasants] will do anything and everything for money!"

It was 1869 and the affluent Taylor family was taking an extended, three-and-a-half-year journey around Europe. Young Fred Taylor observed his father employ the power of his purse to expedite travel—in particular, to get "reluctant local laborers to repair a bridge so the family's touring could proceed." With this formative experience, the basic principle of ***scientific management*** *was born at a bridge in Europe, destined to be transported tumultuously to the corporations of America.*

The operative word here is ***"management":*** *"to control or direct as with the management of a horse." To be sure, Taylor would expand and expound this basic principle of management throughout his life. Taylor sought "the high ground" on behalf of the common workmen. He advocated for just compensation:*

> *"Men will not do an extraordinary day's work for an ordinary day's pay."*

He relieved the workmen of the burden of initiative:

> *"All we want of them is to obey the orders we give them, do what we want, and do it quick."*

He even promoted the workmen's "horse-like" qualities:

> *"I have you for your strength and mechanical ability, and we have other men paid for thinking."*

In the process, Taylor transferred all responsibilities for thinking from the common workmen to the new management class.

For this, Peter Drucker ranks Taylor as responsible for "the most powerful as well as the most lasting contribution America has made to Western thought since the Federalist Papers.*" But Drucker, the enduring journalist, should know better. After having observed the management structure of the Nazi organization in Europe, he was able to identify almost instantaneously the same management systems in the ascending American corporations.*

Certainly, scientific management became the platform of choice for all twentieth-century management theorists, and it has implications for meeting the requirements of the twenty-first-century global marketplace. We will consider those implications later on, but for now, let us return to "the video" we have just seen and view the tape again from another frame of reference.

> *For years, the peasants in Europe had been dismantling bridges in anticipation of affluent travelers just like the Taylors. The peasants did so because they were saving money to come to America, where they would be free of "the burden of the aristocracy." So what better way than to charge the aristocracy for the trip? Thus, on that fateful day in 1869, a group of local peasants were waiting "reluctantly" by the roadside as the elder Taylor "eagerly" raised his bids for their services.*

What is the purpose of these two scenarios? They tell the stories of two different "sciences." The first story is told from a frame of reference external to that of the workers; we can regard this as the manager's frame of reference. The elder Mr. Taylor is brought to a halt at a broken bridge and proceeds to employ his "science" to deal with the situation: he describes *the peasant laborers and their "reluctant" attitude toward work; he* predicts *the incentive power of his money to mobilize them to save his family; he* controls *their actions by negotiating "an extraordinary day's pay for an extraordinary day's work." In so doing, Mr. Taylor manipulates the behavior of the "reluctant" workers, initiating the paradigm for twentieth-century management.*

That is the simplicity of Taylor's "science": describing, predicting, controlling. *These are the functions of* ***the science of probabilities.*** *It is a science dedicated to reducing the variability of any phenomena—people, data, or things—in order to control them.*

The second story is told from the workers' internal frame of reference. We can almost hear their voices:

> *"We'd been taking the bridge down for generations. Up and down! From father to son! Had a few laughs waiting for these bloody aristocrats to come along wanting our help. Got to be pretty good at it. Knew the lynchpins. Got so we could rebuild it as quickly as we could tear it down."*

To "get" this story, we must relate *to the workers' frame of reference: they were setting a trap for the unsuspecting aristocrats. We must also understand their sense of* empowerment *in refining the tools of their trade: they had become quite expert in building and dismantling the bridge. Finally, we must* release *these empowered people to exercise free choice: after "soaking the suckers," they were free to go to America and become anything they chose to be—even bridge builders.*

This is the simplicity of the science that eluded Taylor and his lot: relating, empowering, freeing. *These are the functions of* ***the science of possibilities.*** *It is a science dedicated to relating with all phenomena, including people, in order to empower and free them to make their own unique and continuously changing contributions.*

When they stood on the banks of the river in 1869, the Taylors and the peasants failed to see the symbolism of the bridge. They failed to recognize that beyond their differences was a shared future. They did not see the full value of each other's differences.

Today, we can witness managers playing the key role in interdependent processing as they relate different sources of value to achieve business objectives. From policymaking and strategic processing to organizing and systematizing, management is becoming "process conscious." *Managers have become the "bridge builders," linking our different pasts to our mutual futures.*

PROBABILITIES AND POSSIBILITIES

This is a book about possibilities leaders. Possibilities leaders are managers who process to create whole new ways of doing things. This book explains how they "do" such processing—what kinds of skills, knowledge, and attitudes enable them to be creative.

This is also a story of two marketplace curves: **the probabilities curve** and **the possibilities curve.**

Within **the probabilities curve,** exemplary managers do everything **by the book.** They develop consensus for **best practices.** They set goals, design systems, develop plans, supervise implementation, and evaluate the level of goal achievement. In other words, **they aspire to do things right!**

In this context, we term these exemplars "probabilities managers." Such managers operate according to the assumptions of the science of probabilities. It is a science dedicated to reducing the variability or range of performance of any phenomena—whether our tasks-at-hand or the people performing them. The central purpose of probabilities management is to control everything.

The exemplary probabilities performer operates within the probabilities curve as illustrated in Figure 1-1. It is the exemplar's positioning at the front of the curve that influences other people to aspire to higher performance. The exemplary probabilities performer is the best performer available. This is the level of performance to which all aspire.

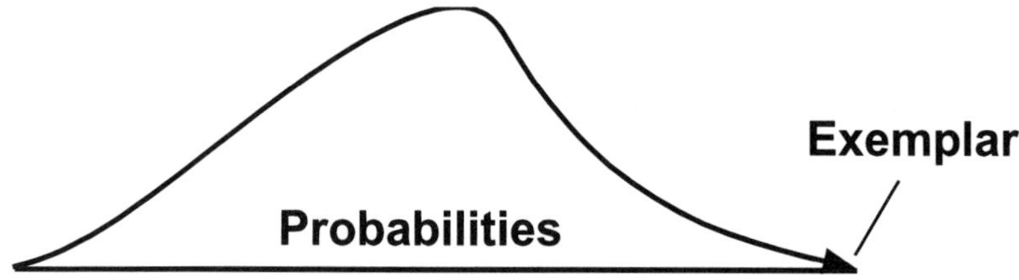

Figure 1-1. Exemplary Probabilities Manager in the Current Performance Curve

In **the possibilities curve,** the managers do not necessarily do everything **by the book.** To be sure, they will use **the book** when it is appropriate. More often than not, they will **write their own book.** Tailored to functional requirements, they will innovate with **best ideas** rather than **best practices.** That is because they can generate with the **best processes.** In other words, **they aspire to do the right thing!**

These possibilities managers are processing people. They operate according to the assumptions of the science of possibilities. It is a science dedicated to expanding the diversity or changeability in the performance of any phenomena.

Possibilities managers are qualitatively different from probabilities managers. At the simplest level, probabilities managers **plan,** while possibilities managers **process.** The major difference may be summarized in the phrase **"continuous and interdependent generative processing."**

Possibilities managers operate outside the commonly accepted performance curve (see Figure 1-2). Indeed, they define entirely new standards for performance, and thus form a new curve. Possibilities managers begin initiating a new curve by generating more productive images of performance.

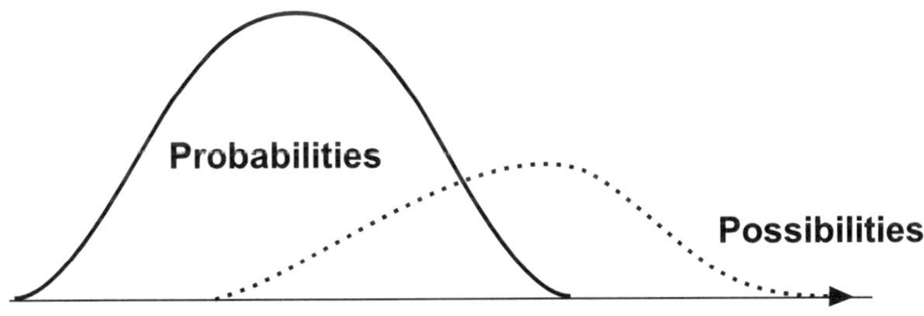

Figure 1-2. Possibilities Manager in a New Performance Curve

Probabilities management is based upon a vision of nature and its processes as *finite.* This limited vision supports the essential, culminating function of such management: to control phenomena. As depicted in Figure 1-3, probabilities management funnels the description and prediction of phenomena into controlling purposes.

It telescopes the contributions of prediction and description to serve humankind's grandiose ambition of controlling all phenomena. Consequently, it seeks and finds less and less variability in performance. Sooner or later, the narrowing of variability results in dysfunctionality or even chaos when new phenomena are introduced or old phenomena change.

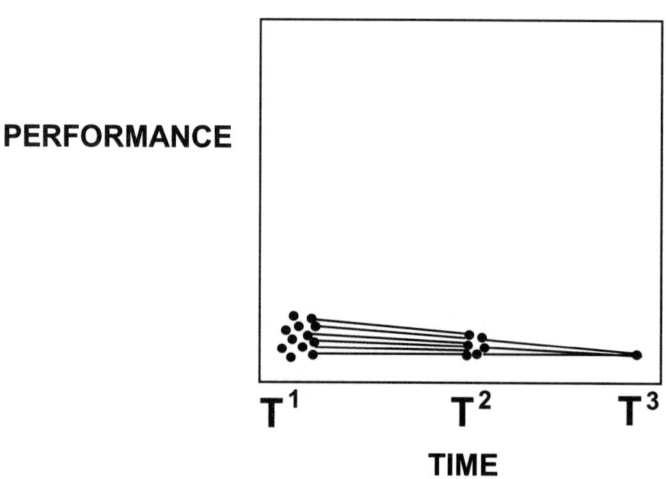

Figure 1-3. Probabilities Management Controls Performance

Possibilities management, in contrast, is based upon a vision of nature and its processes as *continuously changing and growing.* With this expanded vision, possibilities management seeks to relate to phenomena, empower them, and then free their unique contributions. As depicted in Figure 1-4, once phenomena are empowered, they explode in a diversity of changeable dimensionality and performance. Through its possibilities processing systems, possibilities management discovers more and more about more and more phenomena and their changeability.

Managers today are usually dealing with probabilities. They make things happen. They do so by narrowing their focus and narrowing the tolerances of their standards. That is precisely how they have produced products and delivered services through the decades.

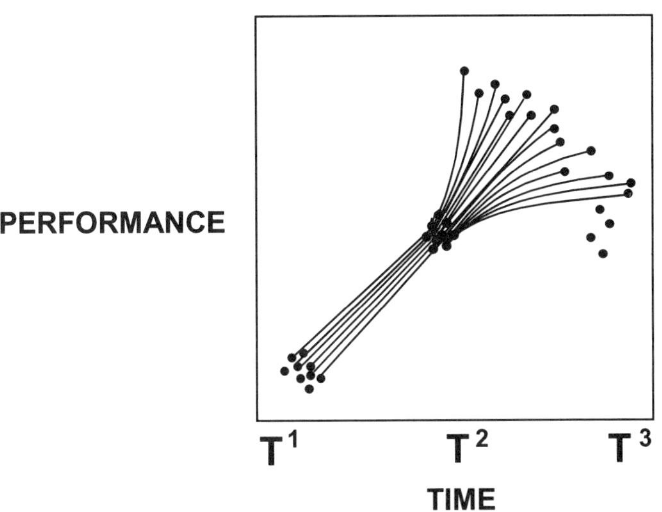

Figure 1-4. Possibilities Management Frees Performance

We find a hierarchy of functions within the traditional organization. The policymakers position the organization in the marketplace. The executives "architect" the organization to implement the positioning. Managers design the systems to achieve organizational goals. Supervisors monitor the implementation of programs to achieve systems objectives. Delivery people perform the tasks to produce products or deliver the services.

Relatedly, we find a similar hierarchy of management processes for accomplishing these organizational responsibilities. The policymakers analyze the data about the marketplace. The executives take this direction and establish organizational goals. The managers receive the handoffs from the executives, define operational goals, and design the systems to achieve them. Then supervisors define the objectives and delivery people produce the products and deliver the services. At least in principle, this is a powerful probabilities management system: every stage of management focuses more precisely upon the end-products. Indeed, the management of probabilities worked very well for us during the twentieth century. Very well! So why should we change now?

To be sure, change is the issue! The problem is that things are changing. The changes are spiraling! The effects are mind-numbing! Probabilities management cannot handle these changes anymore. It cannot handle these changes because it attempts to control them.

We simply cannot control what is inherently changeable. We *can* relate to changes and align with them. We *can* enable changes by empowering them. We *can* release the changes and free them. But we cannot control them!

The mission of control has been a function of humankind's grandiosity. It is an illusion. It assumes that all phenomena are essentially independent and therefore can be isolated and controlled. This is the culminating function of probabilities science—control, control, control!

The mission of freeing phenomena proceeds from our growing awareness of the essential interdependency of all phenomena. This means that changes in any phenomenon generate changes in all phenomena. This is the culminating function of possibilities science—free, free, free!

These are the fundamental differences between probabilities management and possibilities management.

- Probabilities are dedicated to controlling phenomena.
- Possibilities are dedicated to releasing the changeability of phenomena.

There is, of course, a place for controlling phenomena. When we want to produce products with the tightest tolerances and deliver services at the highest current standards of excellence, then we must employ probabilities management. **We must do things right!**

However, when we want to elevate our products and services to deliver more highly leveraged benefits with still more cheaply resourced expenditures, then we must employ possibilities management. **We must do the right thing!**

POSSIBILITIES MANAGEMENT PARADIGM

This book is about freeing managers to enter the realm of possibilities. In order to free managers, we must empower them. And to empower them, we must first relate to them!

By freeing managers in this way, we also free the phenomena they address—their daily tasks, their goals, their problems. Indeed, we free all of these by expanding the functions of managers to include an understanding of policymaking and executive decision-making as well as supervision and delivery issues. We deliver to managers entire databases, and empower them to process creatively at all levels of organizational functions.

We begin to free managers to possibilities when we relate to them and empower them with an understanding of the systems and skills of a new and powerful possibilities management paradigm. The power of that paradigm can be found in its two basic ingredients: **interdependent processing systems** and **organizational management functions.**

Interdependent Processing Systems

The systems of possibilities management may be introduced as follows:

- I^1—Information relating systems,
- I^2—Information representing systems,
- I^3—Individual processing systems,
- I^4—Interpersonal processing systems,
- I^5—Interdependent processing systems.

These are the systems for learning to process interdependently with organizational phenomena.

Information Relating Systems

The fundamental precondition for all possibilities management is defining the operations of phenomena. We relate to phenomena in order to define their operations—to see the world through the eyes of the phenomena, so to speak. Every experience or task has a life. We must define the operations of that life before we can represent it or process with it. A great deal more about these ***information relating systems*** will be presented in Chapter 2.

Information Representing Systems

We relate to phenomena and define phenomenal operations so that we can represent phenomena. We represent phenomena by *imaging* them—representing them multidimensionally. In so doing, we represent not only *what is,* but also the potential for *what can be.* You will learn much more about ***information representing systems*** in Chapter 3.

Individual Processing Systems

By incorporating these information-modeling systems into our individual processing systems, we generate more powerful images of phenomena. In individual processing, we process interdependently with the phenomena themselves as well as with the conditions in which they operate and the standards that they generate. We will take an in-depth look at these ***individual processing systems*** in Chapter 4.

Interpersonal Processing Systems

By incorporating the individual processing systems into our interpersonal processing systems, we generate the most powerful images of phenomena. We process interdependently with the phenomena and interpersonally with other processors. You will learn more about ***interpersonal processing systems*** in Chapter 5.

Interdependent Processing Systems

By incorporating individual and interpersonal processing systems to relate interdependently to phenomenal processing systems, we generate the most powerful images of the phenomena—and ourselves. You will learn more about ***interdependent processing systems*** in Chapter 6.

Together, these processing systems constitute ***the interdependent processing systems of possibilities management*** (see Figure 1-5). Here we have presented the systems developmentally; however, it is important to emphasize that they are *interdependently related.* This means that we may enter them at any phase of development and activate all other phases.

We label these cumulative interdependent processing systems "**I^5**." I^5 processing systems are the basic building blocks of ***possibilities management systems.*** I^5 systems enable managers to discharge their essential organizational management function: the development of new capital. In Chapter 7 we will discuss how I^5 defines process-centric growth.

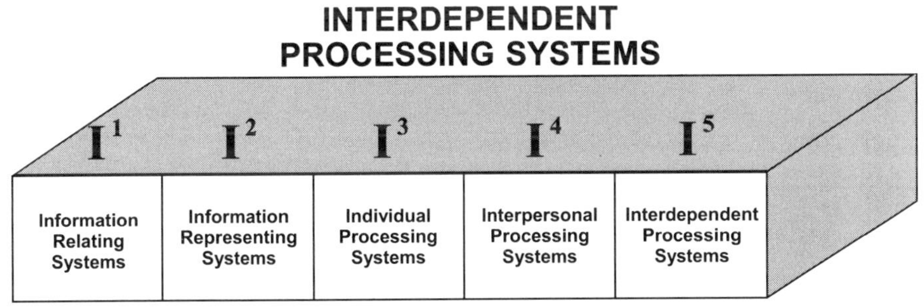

Figure 1-5. Interdependent Processing Systems

Organizational Management Functions

Just as we *"mapped-in"* our interdependent processing systems, we will now *"map-in"* our organizational management functions (or responsibilities). We term these organizational functions *"new capital development systems"* because they describe what is most important to generating wealth in an organization. There are five new capital development (NCD) systems, or organizational functions:

- Marketplace capital development, or MCD;
- Organizational capital development, or OCD;
- Human capital development, or HCD;
- Information capital development, or ICD;
- Mechanical capital development, or mCD.

Let's take a closer look.

Marketplace Capital Development

The first and most important of these management functions is responsibility for managing the organization's positioning in the marketplace. This means managing systems for how the organization continuously differentiates itself for present and future growth in the marketplace. We label marketplace positioning ***"marketplace capital development."***

Organizational Capital Development

Once we have positioned the organization in the marketplace, we need to align the organization with this positioning. This means managing a continuous organizational realignment process to implement constantly changing positioning. We label organizational alignment ***"organizational capital development."***

Human Capital Development

Directed by our organizational alignment, we need to empower our people to process generatively. This means managing processes for the development and support of people to perform continuous interdependent processing of organizational alignment functions. We label this interdependent human processing ***"human capital development."***

Information Capital Development

Empowered by human processing, we need to model our information to serve interdependent and synergistic human processing functions. This means managing processes for the continuous and concurrent modeling of phenomena. We label information modeling ***"information capital development."***

Mechanical Capital Development

Finally, enabled by information modeling, we need to tailor our tools as directed by information modeling so they fulfill information designs and support generative processing. This means managing systems to support the rapid prototyping of tools to meet the personalized requirements of users. We label mechanical tooling ***"mechanical capital development."***

Together, these systems constitute our ***organizational management functions*** (see Figure 1-6). We may use our interdependent processing systems to generatively service these organizational functions. As cumulative systems, these functions are also labeled *"new capital development systems"* or *"NCD systems."*

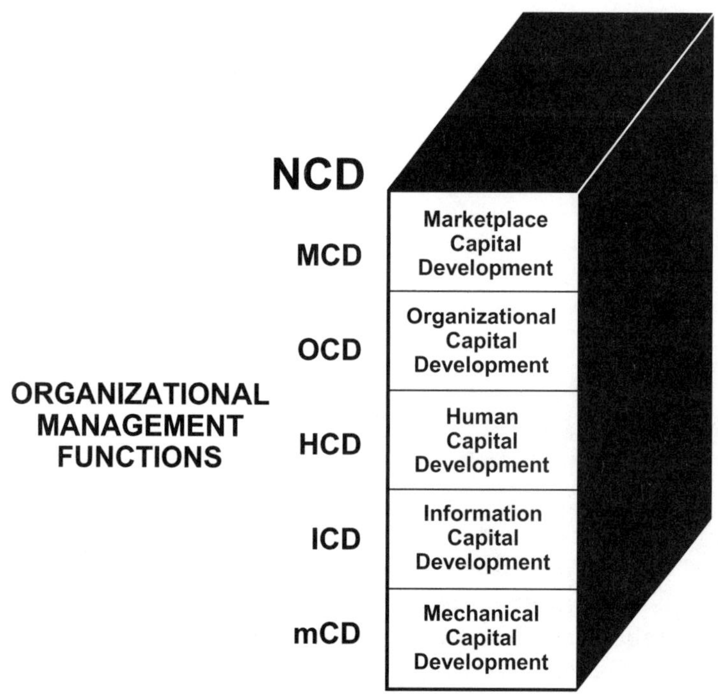

Figure 1-6. Organizational Management Functions

We may summarize the contributions of our possibilities management paradigm as *process-centric growth.* Interdependent processing systems generate NCD and implement NCD initiatives; NCD generates interdependent processing systems. Together, they define process-centric economic growth, a subject we will return to later in this book.

The possibilities management paradigm is represented in Figure 1-7. Here we can clearly see our two basic ingredients: *interdependent processing systems* (which compose the possibilities management systems) and *organizational management functions.* As may be noted, the interdependent processing systems discharge organizational management functions, or NCD. You will learn about variations of this paradigm in chapters to come.

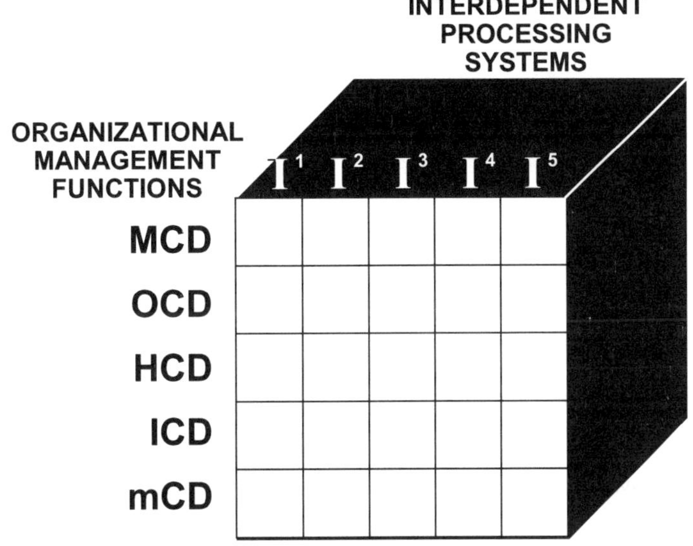

Figure 1-7. The Possibilities Management Paradigm

The possibilities management paradigm is not only the paradigm for this book, but the paradigm for the management of *all* possibilities. When we implement interdependent processing systems at the highest levels, we are functioning as *possibilities leaders*—we are generating new and powerful phenomenal possibilities and innovating in new and potent ways within these possibilities. When we utilize our interdependent processing systems to generate new capital development at all levels of organizational management functions, we are generating and innovating in *the possibilities organization.*

II

The I^5 Possibilities Management Systems

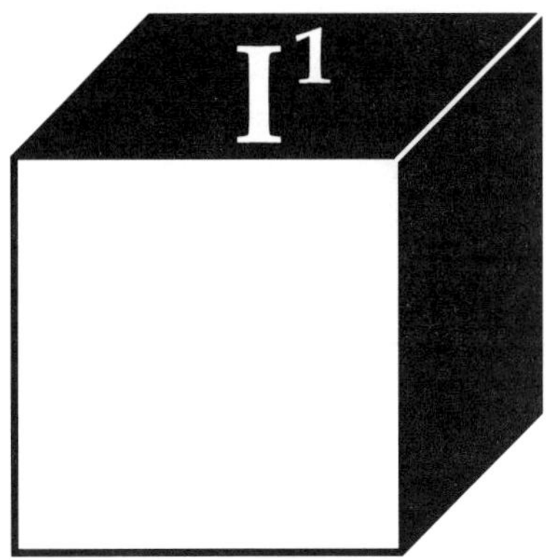

2 I¹—Information Relating Systems

Information relating is the source of all phenomenal operations.

Information modeling is the key to all human processing. Information modeling enables us to represent images of the phenomena, or entities, that we are addressing in our processing. However, before we can model information, we must *relate to* information. Yes, we must relate to data as if it were alive, for indeed it *is* alive! We must transform data into conceptual information that describes our images conceptually in terms of their relationships. Finally, we must transform our conceptual images into operational images that define the phenomena in terms of their operations. Remember, operational definitions enable us to represent the information in multidimensional information models.

Case: The Possibilities Leader
— I^1 Information Relating

Throughout Part II of this book, we will track the progress and growth of a possibilities leader, Sharon Fisher, as she engages in I^5 interdependent processing with her organization. The function of concern is to empower the organization for processing in the twenty-first-century global economy. This processing was undertaken developmentally, or inductively, and exemplifies but one approach to the possibilities management systems.

As C.O.O. of Human Technology, Inc., Sharon Fisher understood the importance of the company's marketplace positioning (see Figure 2-1). She knew the company was positioned to maximize its comparative advantage in the marketplace. She also knew that such market-driven positioning required a flexible and *"super-responsive"* organization dedicated to responding to subtle changes in the marketplace; in short, that it required a *"possibilities organization"* aligned to implement marketplace positioning.

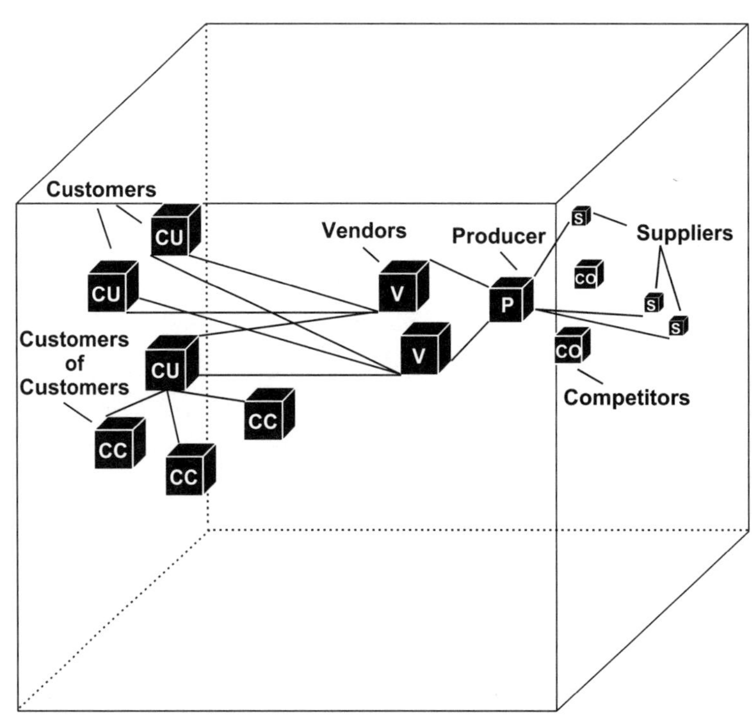

Figure 2-1. Marketplace Positioning

In this context, Fisher had an image of the operational definitions she needed to generate through relating. She defined the operations generically:

- **Functions,** or purposes or outputs;
- **Components,** or parts or inputs;
- **Processes,** or procedures or methods;
- **Conditions,** or contexts or environments;
- **Standards,** or levels of achievement or excellence.

Well aware that she also needed to know the organization well enough to tailor these operational definitions, Fisher related to the organizational experience in order to define its operations. Her initial operational definition is shown next, in Table 2-1.

Table 2-1. Operational Definition of Organization

COMPONENTS	Organizational units are "architected"
FUNCTIONS	to align with marketplace positioning
PROCESSES	by implementing human processing
CONDITIONS	in the context of marketplace requirements
STANDARDS	at uniform standards of human performance.

Fisher was pleased with this definition: it recognized that organizations are built to align with marketplace positions; it also emphasized that organizational functions are implemented by human processing. However, she was concerned about the limitations of her definition for the organization. It did not take into consideration the continuously changing marketplace requirements; therefore, it did not define the organization's continuously changing operations. Accordingly, Fisher continued her relating, and penetrated to a deeper and more powerful level of definition (see Table 2-2).

Table 2-2. New Operational Definition of Organization

COMPONENTS	Organizational units are continuously "architected"
FUNCTIONS	to align with continuous marketplace positioning
PROCESSES	by implementing continuous interdependent processing
CONDITIONS	in the context of spiraling marketplace requirements
STANDARDS	at increasingly diverse and changeable standards of human processing and information modeling.

> As can be seen, Fisher gave the operational definition a whole new meaning—intentionality! The organization is defined by continuous alignment with continuous changes in marketplace requirements and positioning; by continuous interdependent processing with increasingly diverse and changeable standards of performance.

INFORMATION RELATING SYSTEMS

The goal of information relating is to produce operational images of phenomena (see Figure 2-2). In other words, we transform conceptual images into operational images. We build operational images by defining conceptual information in operational terms. (Operational definitions of anything mean that we can act upon those definitions.) These operations-defining skills may be labeled *"information relating skills."* As shown in Figure 2-2, conceptual information is represented in a linear manner: facts, concepts, principles, applications, objectives. In turn, operational information defines the concepts as functions, components, processes, conditions, standards. The entire process for transforming conceptual information into operational information is accomplished by our information relating, or I^1, systems.

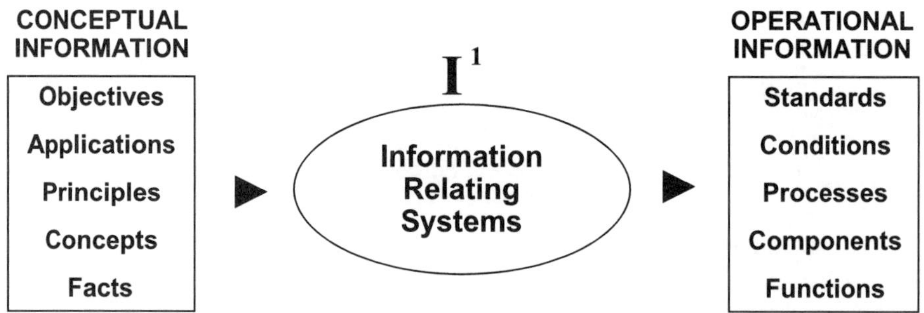

Figure 2-2. Information Relating Systems

The relationship between human processing and information modeling is interdependent and synergistic. Human processing generates information models: the quality of information is precisely how we can discriminate the quality of human processing. High-quality information modeling thus enables high-quality human processing. Moreover, it is essential to information capital: the information modeling that is *"most important"* to our processing mission. Indeed, the quality of information modeling defines information capital.

In turn, information modeling generates human processing: the quality of human processing is precisely how we can discriminate the quality of information modeling. High-quality human processing thus enables high-quality information modeling. Moreover, it is essential to human capital: the human processing that is *"most important"* to our processing mission. To be sure, the quality of human processing defines human capital.

In possibilities management, we introduce this interdependent and synergistic relationship with our information relating systems. The systems of human processing, or human capital development (HCD), begin to build the systems of information modeling, or information capital development (ICD):

HCD ⟷ ICD

In turn, the ICD systems begin to build the HCD systems. This marks the earliest phase of possibilities management, when information relating skills transform conceptual information into operational information.

Relating: An Introduction

Terry was a bold and powerful general manager of a manufacturing division. Because he had presented to all of the audiences within his organization and to those in many customer organizations, he felt that he had a *"finger on the pulse of the people."* He had listened and "heard" their aspirations and concerns. He had rewarded them empathically for their efforts. Consequently, he oversaw many of the marketing initiatives to discern customer needs. Often he vetoed these initiatives because he "knew" what customers needed. The problem was, *he really didn't know anything!*

Many people mistake communicating for relating. This is particularly the case when people—especially managers—communicate *to* others rather than *with* them. This "Reaganesque" or "Clintonesque" behavior is more like a presentation or a performance: a one-way communication to *spin* one's message or demonstrate one's expertise to others.

We can easily see why this kind of communicating has nothing to do with relating. It does not merge with the experience of the audience. It does not describe people's needs in operational terms. It does not, therefore, make the responses to their needs achievable.

When we analyze "the great communicators," we usually find that, contrary to appearance, they have quite limited skills at relating. Because they discuss the same themes with so many audiences, they may have a comprehensive grasp of certain issues and so *seem* to relate to people and their needs; yet, almost without exception, they relate only to conceptual information, and only at the levels of facts and concepts. Rarely do they discriminate the principles that explain the relationships between concepts. Consequently, they may develop prime conceptual information—concepts that incorporate the issues most inclusively. But they almost never develop operational information—operations that define achievable objectives and do so systematically.

At best, the facts and concepts that are input may be transformed into prime facts and concepts at output. Again, this may be helpful for purposes of carrying forward the corporate message: the communicators sharpen their delivery of vivid concepts to the audience. However, these communications are not to be confused with learning something about the customers' operational needs. In short, the communicators are conceptualizers rather than operationalizers. They are conceptualizing to persuade, rather than operationalizing to achieve.

Conceptual Information

The objective of relating is to transform conceptual information into useable, or operational, information. Except at the objective level, the various levels of conceptual information cannot be acted upon. They merely state relationships within, between, and among phenomena.

In building levels of conceptual information, we may be guided by the traditional definitions shown in Table 2-3 and detailed below.

- **Facts**—The *labels* we attach to phenomena;
- **Concepts**—The *relationships* between phenomena;
- **Principles**—The *explanations* of these relationships between phenomena;
- **Applications**—The *contexts* for the demonstrations of the phenomena;
- **Objectives**—The *operations* of the demonstrations of the phenomena.

Note that only at the highest level of conceptual information do we begin to define operational information.

Table 2-3. Levels of Conceptual Information

OBJECTIVES:	**Operations of phenomena**
APPLICATIONS:	**Contexts for phenomena**
PRINCIPLES:	**Explanations for phenomena**
CONCEPTS:	**Relationships between phenomena**
FACTS:	**Labels attached to phenomena**

Perhaps more than 99 percent of the information generated and communicated is conceptual. In general, conceptual information relates two or more entities. They may be data points or facts that we connect. We may provide explanations for these relationships in the form of principles. We may even direct these relationships in making applications. Finally, we may define objectives for making applications.

Relating to Conceptual Information

In time, Terry became aware of his limited ability at relating and set out to learn more about conceptual information. He found educators who were experts in cognitive learning. They explained that there were five levels of conceptual information: facts, concepts, principles, applications, and objectives. Terry began to see that all of these levels emphasized the relationships between phenomena—whether people, data, or things. This understanding was a confidence-builder for him.

Equipped with his new knowledge, Terry went out on the road. He delivered an entry learning experience on discriminating the levels of conceptual information. Starting at **the level of facts,** he taught his audiences how to label entities such as people, data, and things. Then he asked them whether it was possible *to act* upon what they had learned. Invariably, audiences answered with a resounding *"No!"* So much for factual information!

Terry focused next on **the level of concepts,** delivering his insights on the relationships between and among factual entities—people, data, things. Again he asked his audiences whether it was possible *to act* upon what they had learned. *"No!"* responded one audience after another, although many people found concepts more interesting than facts. Soon Terry concluded that concepts were quite limited in terms of usefulness.

The next topic was **the level of principles.** Terry made clear that principles were explanations for the relationships between entities. To audiences, principles had meaning because they defined how things worked. Nonetheless, people did not find this level *"action-able";* they still felt unable *to act* upon conceptual information.

The level of applications was particularly interesting to audiences. They became involved in Terry's illustrations of the contexts, or environments, in which relationships between entities were implemented. The illustrations were vivid to people—they could relate these to real-life applications! However, that did not make this level any more *action-able* to them than the other levels had been.

It was not until Terry explained **the level of objectives** that his audiences really caught on. Objectives were defined by the operations involved in applications, and also specified standards. People concluded that *the definition of operations* was what made objectives achievable. This was indeed an *action-able* level of information.

Terry learned a great deal from his road experience. He now had a clear image of his objectives in relating: to discriminate and communicate at *the level of operations.* The more he could transform the conceptual into the operational, the more his audiences would receive something to which they could relate—something useful, *action-able,* achievable.

It was not long before Terry decided to learn more about operations. We will return to that part of his story shortly.

Most people communicate at the lowest levels of conceptual information: facts and concepts are, at best, transformed into prime statements of conceptual relationships. Very few people ever search out the principles, or the explanations, for the relationships. Still fewer can identify the contexts for applications. Without training, none can identify the objectives or operations. Yet it is the definition of operations that makes the objectives achievable.

Operational Information

Operational images of phenomena thus bring conceptual information to life. They make conceptual information "action-able." They allow phenomena to act or to be acted upon and so empower phenomena with a fullness of life, or "lifefulness."

In building levels of operations, we are guided by the traditional definitions shown in Table 2-4 and detailed below.

- **Functions**—The *outputs* we wish to achieve;
- **Components**—The *inputs* we are willing to invest;
- **Processes**—The *procedures* required to transform inputs into outputs;
- **Conditions**—The *contexts* within which the processing takes place;
- **Standards**—The *levels of achievement* by which we measure our success.

These operations will enable us to define conceptual information operationally.

Table 2-4. Levels of Operational Information

STANDARDS:	**Levels of achievement or excellence**
CONDITIONS:	**Contexts or environments**
PROCESSES:	**Methods or procedures**
COMPONENTS:	**Parts or participants or inputs**
FUNCTIONS:	**Purposes or products or outputs**

We may also view operations from the perspective of basic interrogatives:

- **Functions**—*What* is being done?
- **Components**—*Who* and *what* are doing it?
- **Processes**—*How* are they doing it?
- **Conditions**—*Where* and *when* and *why* are they doing it?
- **Standards**—*How well* are they doing it?

Relating to Operational Information

Terry now realized that the highest level of conceptual information was defined by operational information; or, to put it more simply, that objectives were defined by operations. He resolved to conquer the operations involved in defining objectives. In other words, his objective in relating was to define objectives.

Terry sought help from his engineers. He knew that everything they designed was operational, and he wanted to know the operations involved. Terry learned there were five important levels of operations:

1. **Functions.** Functions emphasize the outputs, or purposes, of all operations. They are defined by ***what*** we are trying to accomplish. Typically, the requirements for functions are derived from superordinate units; in other words, the higher unit's needs become the subordinate unit's requirements. In this context, functions are usually defined in terms of products and services and sometimes in activities leading to products and services.

2. **Components.** If functions are outputs, then components are inputs. They emphasize the parts or participants needed to discharge the functions. Components are defined by ***who*** and ***what*** are involved in accomplishing the functions.
3. **Processes.** The processes are the means by which the component units are transformed into function outputs. They emphasize the procedures, or methods, involved. Processes are defined by ***how*** the components discharge functions.
4. **Conditions.** These are the higher-order contexts within which the operations are implemented. They emphasize the context, or environment, for the operations. Conditions are defined by ***when*** and ***where*** the operations take place. As superordinate contexts, they may also define the requirements for ***why*** the operations take place.
5. **Standards.** The standards reflect the level of accomplishment. They emphasize measures of the level of achievement, or degree of excellence. They are defined by ***how well*** the operations have performed in accomplishing the functions.

Terry now realized that we relate to phenomenal experiences with a purpose:

> *To transform our concepts* about *things into the operations* of *things; to transform conceptual information into operational information.*

He could now see that conceptualizing was circular—that concepts were defined by relationships, and so conceptually. For the first time, Terry could define conceptual information *operationally*. He had the basic key to such definition:

Transforming Conceptual Information Into Operational Information

- **Facts are defined by components and functions.**
- **Concepts are defined by relationships within, between, and among components and functions.**
- **Principles are defined by processing to transform components into functions.**
- **Applications are defined by the conditions within which the other operations take place.**
- **Objectives are defined by the operations required to accomplish the applications.**

INFORMATION RELATING SKILLS

Possibilities management is first and foremost an empathic science: possibilities managers relate to phenomena in order to merge with phenomena. But this is an empathic science with a purpose! Just as possibilities managers relate to merge, so do they merge to relate to the phenomenal experience. Specifically, they relate to phenomena in order to transform the concepts about the phenomena's experience into operations that can be acted upon.

To empathize with phenomena, then, we must relate to phenomena to transform conceptual information into operational information. When working with people, we engage in what are called *"interpersonal systems."* When working with all phenomena, we engage in what are called *"interrelating systems,"* or *"information relating systems."* In information relating systems, we relate to generate the operations involved. Such systems are represented in Table 2-5.

Table 2-5. Information Relating Systems

CONCEPTUAL INFORMATION \ OPERATIONAL INFORMATION	Functions	Components	Processes	Conditions	Standards
Objectives					
Applications					
Principles					
Concepts					
Facts					

As may be noted, operational information is matrixed with conceptual information. This information matrix yields the following:

- At the lowest level, **facts** (or labels) are defined by components and functions. Components and functions define, respectively, ***who*** and ***what*** are taking part, and ***what*** is taking place. Basically, components are the people, data, and things we invest as input; the functions are the products, services, and solutions we accomplish as outputs.

FACTS: Components, Functions

- At the level of **concepts,** relationships are established within, between, and among phenomena. Thus, for example, components may be related to functions as inputs are related to outputs or as subjects are related to objects in a sentence. Components may also be related to components as, for example, nouns are related to adjectives. Functions may be related to functions as verbs are to adverbs.

CONCEPTS: Components ⟶ Functions

- At the level of **principles,** processing systems define ***how*** the relationships between phenomena exist. For example, processes transform the components into functions; the modifying components of components; the modifying functions of functions. In so doing, the processing systems not only transform the phenomena but also explain the phenomenal relationship.

PRINCIPLES: Components ⟶ Processes ⟶ Functions

- The **applications** are defined by the conditions within which they operate. The conditions define ***where*** and ***when*** the applications will take place. They also may define ***why*** the applications are being made. In this respect, all processing takes place within the conditions of the applications.

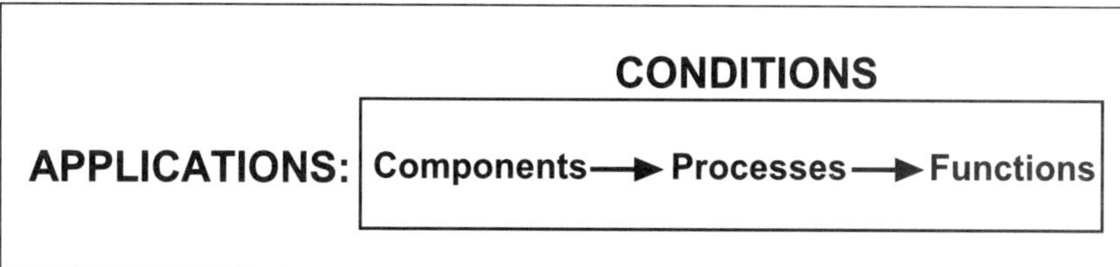

- The **objectives** are defined by all of the operations that define phenomena, including, and especially, standards. The standards provide the feedback on ***how well*** we are doing what we are doing.

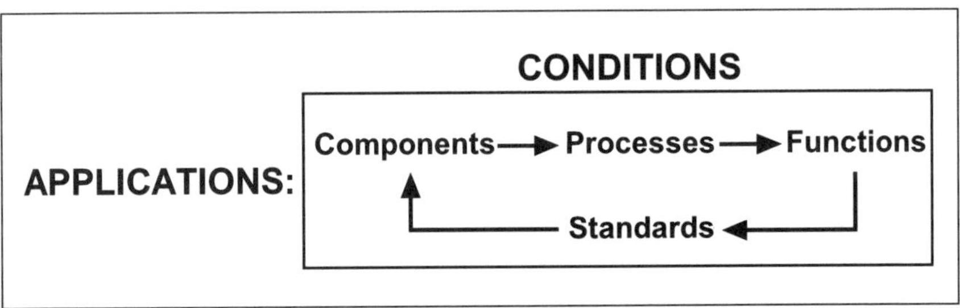

Together, these operations enable us to define the conceptual information operationally (see Table 2-6). Note that the highest level of conceptual information is defined by a fully operational processing system:

> *Components are transformed into functions by processing systems under specifiable conditions with measurable standards.*

Table 2-6. Levels of Operational Information

CONCEPTUAL LEVELS	
OBJECTIVES:	CONDITIONS Components → Processes → Functions (Functions → Standards → Components)
APPLICATIONS:	CONDITIONS Components → Processes → Functions
PRINCIPLES:	Components → Processes → Functions
CONCEPTS:	Components → Processes
FACTS:	Components, Functions

All of this prepares us for building operational information in which all levels of all conceptual information are defined by all operations: components, functions, processes, conditions, standards.

We may illustrate operational information with examples of people:

> *People perform tasks by thinking systematically at individual workstations at definable performance standards.*

Similarly, we may illustrate with data examples:

> *Data is transformed into information by model-building at individual workstations at replicable levels.*

Likewise, we may illustrate with organizational examples:

> *Organizational units implement continuous alignment by continuous human processing under changing marketplace conditions with diverse and changing levels of standards.*

In summary, operational information makes conceptual information *action-able.* Operationalizing generates the operations of phenomena. They constitute the purpose of relating.

Relating-Skills Training

True phenomenal relators are powerful, but they are rarely found on the work scene. To become relators, people need to be systematically trained in relating skills or mentored by exemplars. Indeed, in Terry's case, such training made all the difference. It helped him see how inadequate his communicating had been, and gave him a solid base for growth and improvement.

Through training, Terry discovered there were specific sets of skills for relating: attending, responding, personalizing, and initiating. These skills would enable him to respond to an audience's frames of reference—to see the world through people's eyes. Moreover, these relating skills would empower him to do the following:

- Personalize people's experiences, particularly in terms of deficits in operating;
- Individualizing those experiences while initiating courses of action to generate assets in operating.

In short, Terry could learn to relate to merge with the experiences of his audience.

The relating skills and their definitions helped Terry build on what he had learned from engineering. They made clear that the purpose of relating was to transform concepts *about phenomena* into operations *of phenomena.* In this context, Terry noticed that the relating-skills scale was transformed from attending and responding to concepts about phenomena at the lower levels to responding to the operations of phenomena at the higher levels.

Terry's trainer gave him an innovative template for discriminating and communicating with phenomena by employing information relating systems. That template is shown next.

RELATING SKILLS	FORMAT FOR RELATING TO PHENOMENA
INITIATING (Operations)	"You feel ___(AFFECT)___ because you can ___(OPERATIONS ASSETS)___."
PERSONALIZING (Operations)	"You feel ___(AFFECT)___ because you cannot ___(OPERATIONS DEFICITS)___."
RESPONDING (Operations)	"You feel ___(AFFECT)___ because ___(OPERATIONS)___."
RESPONDING (Concepts)	"You said ___(OBJECTIVES)___."
ATTENDING (Concepts)	"You are ___(CONCEPTUAL)___."

As illustrated, the relator responds to the affect (or feeling) of the phenomenal experience and to the operations eliciting this affect. Thus the relator treats the phenomena as living entities—and for our purposes, all phenomena (data and things as well as people) are indeed alive!

Attending

Terry could apply the relating skills most readily with people with whom he worked. For example, in attending, Terry could communicate *"hovering attentiveness"* by *squaring* with, *leaning into,* and *making eye contact* with people. Moreover, attending focused his observing skills. The very message of merging is found in observing: we observe so that we may *see.*

In this context, Terry observed his people from three different frames of reference:

1. He *looked at* their external appearance and behavior to *see* them as they presented themselves to their worlds.
2. He *looked in* to their internal frames of reference to *see* how they saw themselves.

3. He *looked out* to their external frames of reference to *see* the world as they saw it.

In other words, he used his observing skills to *see* his people from different vantage points.

Here is what Terry could *see* as he observed his people:

1. He could *see* them as they presented themselves: conventional and safely set within all social norms.
2. He could *see* them as they saw themselves: vulnerable and fearful of the spiraling changes in business.
3. He could *see* the world as they saw it: as threatening and powerful market forces responding to their own changing requirements.

Terry was surprised that he could *see* most of what he needed to know about his people simply by attending. He was able to summarize it in this way:

> *"You are scared in the face of a fearsome flurry of changes beyond your control."*

Moreover, Terry attended to the levels of conceptual information that his people expressed: facts, concepts, principles, applications, objectives. To do this, he employed the *"5W2H"* formula—*who, what, why, when, where, how, how well?*—in his own systems paradigm:

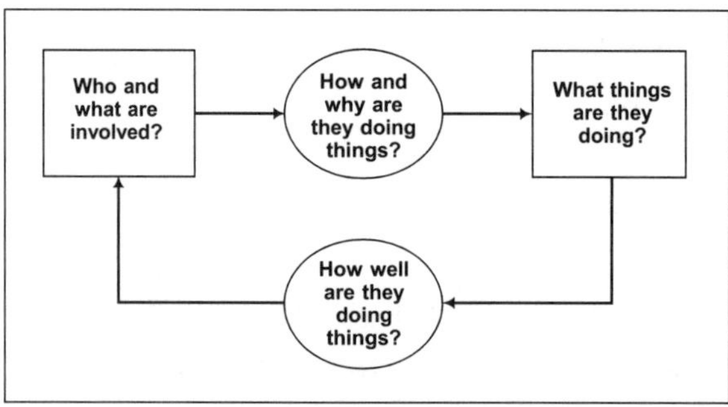

Where and When?

This *"5W2H"* system helped Terry understand what levels of conceptual information were present and what levels of conceptual information were absent. Terry found that most people were unclear about what they were trying to do: what their outputs were. This made all other levels of conceptual information difficult to communicate. Terry responded accordingly:

> *"You're confused about how to address these changes with your current level of knowledge."*

For the first time, Terry began to feel that he could *see* the experience of his people. He had become quite familiar with it himself.

Responding to Concepts

Terry continued relating to his people by applying responding skills. As he soon found out, responding skills build directly upon attending skills. Just as we focus upon observing people in order to *see* them, we focus upon listening to people in order to *hear* them. Just as we have captured their experience by inferring from their appearance and behavior, we now emphasize responding interchangeably with the expressions of their experience.

In responding interchangeably, we communicate our understanding of the phenomena. Whether the phenomena are literally alive or not, we respond to them as if they were alive. By attending, we, as responders, have seen and heard the phenomenal experience. Now we reflect upon these experiences and formulate our responses to the concepts of the expressions of that experience.

For example, in Terry's case, staff members expressed themselves as follows: *"We don't have direction for our day-to-day tasks."* Thus they addressed the *objective* level of conceptual information. Terry decided to probe further, to see whether his staff truly understood the *explanation* and *context* for the procedural tasks involved. He was able to do so through the following response:

> *"You're also saying that you're unsure of the principles and the applications involved."*

In this manner, Terry mapped his responding skills into the expressed levels of conceptual information:

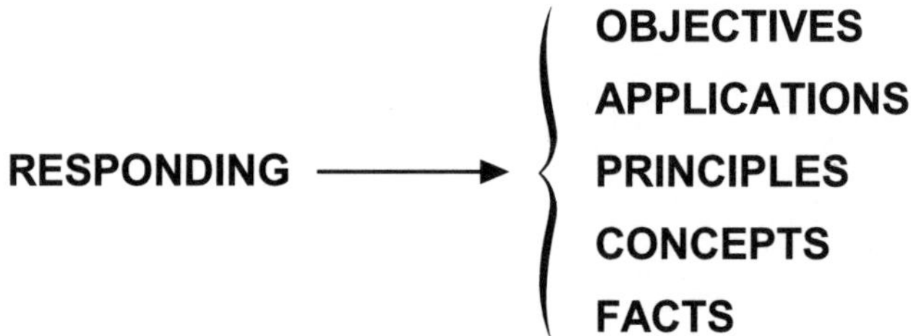

Terry realized that, diagnostically, he could discriminate the levels at which people expressed themselves.

Thus, before we can respond to operations, we must capture the level of conceptual information that has been expressed.

1. If we can repeat an expression verbatim, then we are *interchangeable with* the expression.
2. If we can also discriminate the level of conceptual information expressed, then we are *additive to* the expression.
3. If we cannot discriminate the level of conceptual information expressed, then we are *subtractive from* the expression.

Terry knew these distinctions, and they enabled him to discriminate his own readiness for responding to operations.

Responding to Operations

Responding to operations grows out of continuous and ongoing responding to concepts. For example, Terry continued to respond to his staff members:

> *"You're really saying that you're unsure of all the operations involved in day-to-day tasks."*

This enabled Terry to diagnose his people differentially in terms of their deficits in operating.

Just as Terry had mapped his responding skills into the levels of conceptual information expressed, so he now mapped them into the levels of operational information *not* expressed:

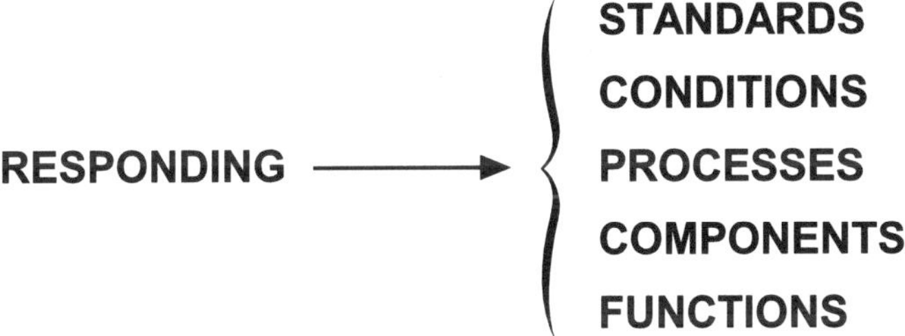

This enabled Terry to discriminate the levels at which people were processing on an ongoing basis.

For example, ongoing interactions revealed that staff members were becoming confident in their understanding of functions, components, and processes; however, they had trouble understanding where the requirements came from. Terry responded appropriately:

> *"You feel uncertain of the conditions for the operations involved."*

This response to operations gave people the opportunity to provide feedback on its accuracy: again, interchangeable, additive, or subtractive. With feedback, Terry found that he could begin to respond to the affective experience involved:

> *"You feel confused about all of the requirements involved in your day-to-day tasks."*

Terry continued to formulate responses in ongoing interactions. He *"zeroed in"* on the true feelings involved:

> *"You really feel angry because I gave you the tasks without standards."*

As Terry discovered, responding to the operations and the resulting feelings is what responding is all about. Responding to operations is the threshold of relating: once we reach it, we have merged with the phenomenal experience; once we cross it, we can generate an operational experience.

Personalizing Operations

Before too long, Terry found that by continuing to respond, he had earned the right to personalize. In responding, we communicate our understanding of phenomenal experience. In personalizing, we help the phenomena to internalize responsibility for their experience: to accept ownership of their shortcomings or deficits in the operations. For instance, Terry personalized the experience of his staff members as follows:

> *"You feel disappointed in yourself because you can't manage the operations."*

Again, this personalizing enabled Terry to diagnose his people differentially in terms of deficits in operating.

Just as Terry had *mapped-in* his responding skills, he now *mapped-in* his personalizing skills, to the levels of operations *"owned"* by his people:

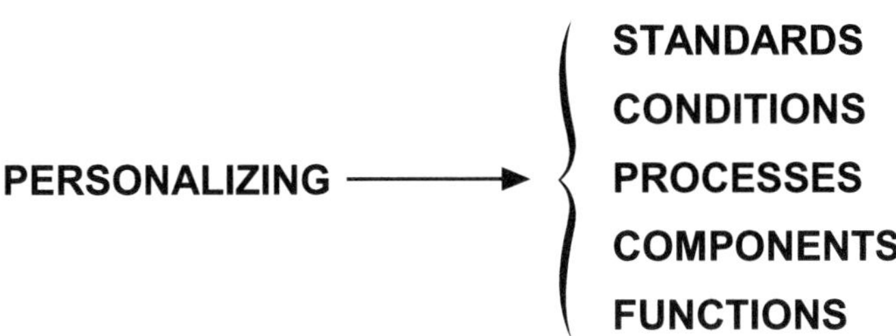

Terry could now discriminate the levels of operations internalized by his people.

For example, Terry's continued responding led to his personalizing the deficits in standards of operations:

> *"You feel disappointed because you cannot understand how your performance will be measured."*

This personalized response internalized the staff's deficits in operations while allowing for feedback regarding its accuracy.

Further personalizing *"pinpointed"* the staff's deficits in assuming responsibility for eliciting this information about standards:

> *"You feel disappointed because you cannot manage to mobilize to meet the requirements."*

This personalized response established the basis for transforming operational deficits into assets.

Personalizing, Terry realized, extends beyond responding because it clarifies an understanding of the possible. We cannot change unless we assume responsibility for our current performance. He made his own personalized response to himself:

> *"I feel disappointed that for so long I made no effort to conquer relating skills."*

Personalizing, Terry concluded, is the soul of change.

Initiating Operations

In personalizing, we enable the phenomena to internalize responsibility for deficits in operations and the responsibility for change. Now, in initiating, we enable the phenomena to transform these deficits into assets in operations. For example, Terry initiated with his staff members as follows:

> *"You feel excited because now you can learn to manage the operations."*

This focused the staff upon learning to develop assets in their operations.

Again, Terry employed mapping. This time he mapped his initiating skills into his people's intended levels of operations:

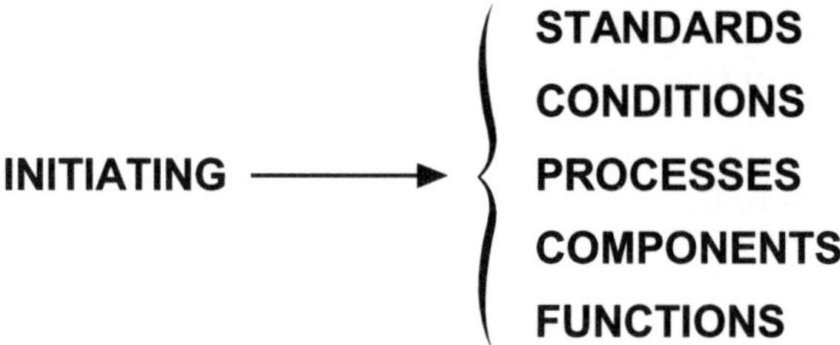

This enabled Terry to collaborate with his staff members to define the operational objectives and then develop programs to achieve those objectives.

Continued personalizing led to Terry's initiating to transform the conditions and standards deficits into assets:

> *"You feel eager to learn how your performance will be measured."*

This initiative response internalized the staff's commitment to acquiring operational assets. Further initiating *"pin-pointed"* the staff's intended operational assets:

> *"You feel confident because you can learn to meet the standards."*
>
> This initiative response allowed Terry and his staff to acquire operational assets by operationally defining their objectives for conditions and standards.
>
> Terry recognized that change culminates with the programs we develop to achieve our operational objectives. He made his own initiative response:
>
> *"I feel excited because we are now initiating the effort to change."*
>
> Terry concluded that change begins with relating, culminates with initiating, and then begins all over again with relating! Since change is spiraling, our growth through relating is spiraling!

SUMMARY AND TRANSITION

In summary, the objective of information relating systems is to transform conceptual information about phenomena into operational information that defines phenomena: functions, components, processes, conditions, standards. The ability to articulate conceptual information and to transform it into operational information is a function of the quality of our information relating skills.

Again, the key to processing is building operational information. With operational information, we can generate true courses of action.

In terms of day-to-day activities, this means that our people are, at a minimum, operational in the information they have defined. Check them out! *What* is being done? *Who* is doing it? *How* are they doing it? *Where, when, why,* and *how well* are they doing it?

A valuable tool for managing I^1 is our information matrix, shown in Table 2-7. With this tool, we may assess our employees' levels of functioning in relation to all phenomena:

1. Factual operations,
2. Conceptual operations,
3. Principles operations,
4. Applications operations,
5. Objectives operations.

Table 2-7. I^1 Management Systems

CONCEPTUAL INFORMATION	OPERATIONAL INFORMATION: Functions	Components	Processes	Conditions	Standards
Objectives					
Applications					
Principles					
Concepts					
Facts					

The answers to our operational-information questions will dictate our level of confidence in any future representations of the phenomena that people may develop. If our people give us evidence of relating, then their images are worthy of consideration. If not, then the images as well as the people must be scrutinized.

Case: The Possibilities Leader (continued)

In returning to our possibilities leader, Sharon Fisher, we find that her efforts in this relating phase were highly successful. Through these efforts, she was able to confirm the following:

1. *All things are possible with relating; nothing is possible without it.* Without relating, there are only probabilities—ultimately, probabilities for failure; with relating, there are potentially infinite possibilities.

   Specifically, the operational information generated by information relating systems enable information representing systems: together, they constitute preparation for processing, serving to introduce managers and phenomena to each other's possibilities.

2. *The power of information relating relies in large part on attitude:* an attitude of humility, to be sure—a recognition that no one has all the answers and that all answers will be discovered by processing with the phenomena!

Moreover, and most important, Fisher concluded that information relating signifies interdependency with our universe—our workstation, team, unit, organization, customers, suppliers, vendors, and marketplace. As we fully enter the twenty-first century, it is clear that no one, and nothing, is independent. Perhaps such independence was only a twentieth-century illusion!

In merging with phenomena, then, we focus our *information relating skills* upon the phenomena and their experiences (see Figure 2-3). This enables us to transform conceptual information into operational information. In turn, the operational information will enable us to represent the phenomena as we prepare for processing. To process, we must have skills in information representing: the skills to model the information dimension of phenomena.

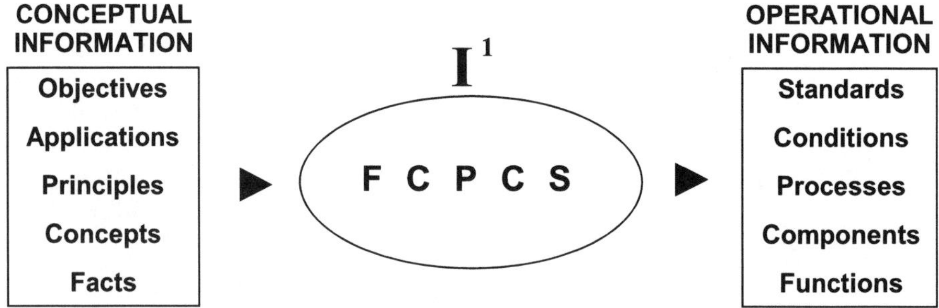

Figure 2-3. Information Relating Systems

Just as we can intervene to respond to people, we can respond to merge with any phenomena. We begin to actualize our contributions by applying our information relating skills with all of the tasks in our daily existence.

In transition, the principle of information relating is that ***everything lives:*** all phenomena are worthy of our relating. If we do not find them worthy of relating, then we are not worthy of relating to them. And none of us will grow!

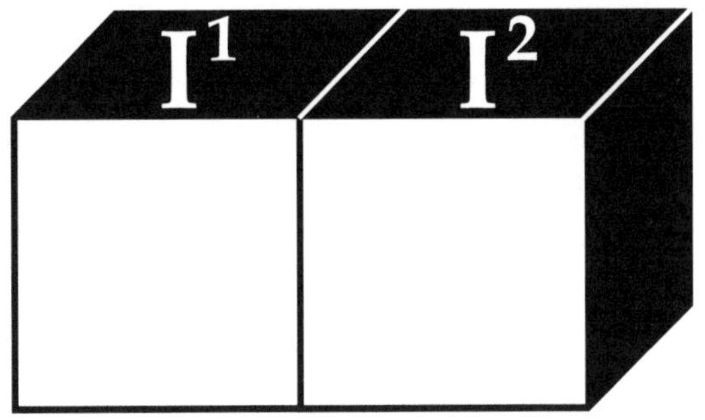

3 I^2—Information Representing Systems

Information representing is the source of all phenomenal imaging.

Our models of information empower us to process information. Indeed, information modeling—not connectivity—is the culmination of information technology. Information modeling enables human technology to process information generatively.

Case: The Possibilities Leader — I^2 Information Representing

Armed with an understanding of the operations of the organization, Sharon Fisher entered the next phase in interdependent processing: building a dimensional image of the organization. She needed to "see" the organization; in particular, she needed to see how every dimension related to every other dimension. Accordingly, Fisher began to "dimensionalize" the operations of the organization.

Our possibilities leader already had a good image of the functions of the organization (see Table 3-1). She understood the functions as follows:

- **Policy** defined the missions to implement marketplace positioning;
- **Executives** designed the organizational architecture to align with marketplace positioning;
- **Management** designed the systems to achieve the goals of organizational alignment;
- **Supervision** defined the objectives to implement the systems;
- **Delivery** performed the tasks required to achieve the objectives.

She now needed to define the resource components that accomplished these functions.

Table 3-1. Organizational Functions

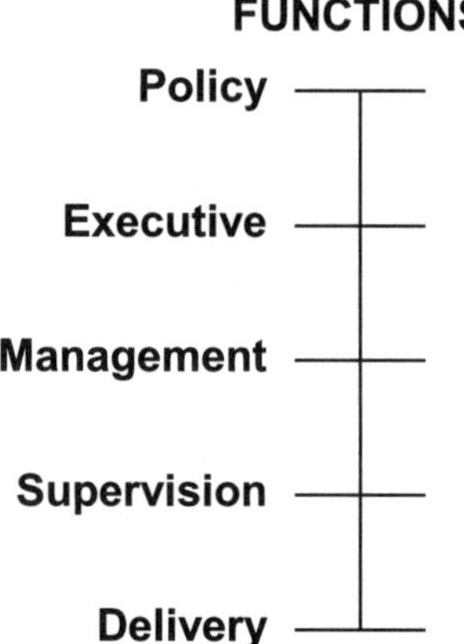

Fisher initiated "dimensionalization" by developing the organizational components that discharged these functions. This development entailed constructing a two-dimensional matrix for defining the organizational components (see Table 3-2). In working with the matrix, Fisher came to understand the components as follows:

- **Leadership** defined the new marketplace directions to reflect marketplace positioning;
- **Marketing** developed new marketing relationships with customers to reflect marketplace directions;
- **Resource integration** developed tailored solutions for customers in new marketing relationships;
- **Technology** developed customized designs for products and services in new marketing relationships;
- **Production** produced standardized products and services in new marketing relationships.

She now needed to define the organizational processes that enabled the components to discharge the functions.

Table 3-2. Organizational Functions and Components

FUNCTIONS \ COMPONENTS	Leadership	Marketing	Resources	Technology	Production
Policy					
Executive					
Management					
Supervision					
Delivery					

Fisher continued to dimensionalize by developing the organizational processes that enabled the components to discharge the functions (see Figure 3-1). She did this by developing a three-dimensional model that defined the organizational processes:

- **Goaling,** or measuring values;
- **Inputting,** or analyzing operations;
- **Processing,** or synthesizing new operations;
- **Planning,** or operationalizing new objectives;
- **Outputting,** or technologizing new programs.

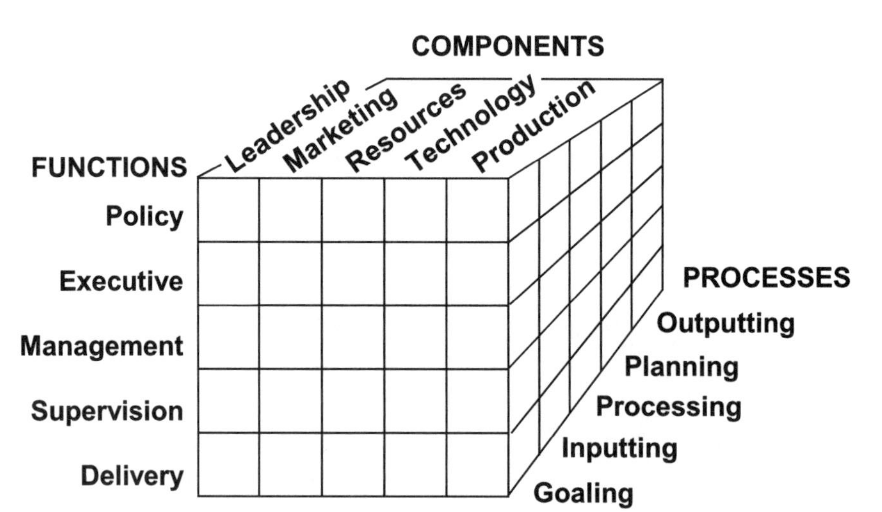

Figure 3-1. Organizational Functions, Components, and Processes

Fisher had now developed a three-dimensional model, and could "see" how every level of every dimension related to every other dimension. This gave her a great perspective on organizational operations. However, she had not dimensionalized all of the operations.

Paramount among the operations were the conditions within which the organization operated (see Figure 3-2). Fisher found that these conditions generated the functions of the organization. As such, they were prepotent factors in organizational functioning.

For the time being, she was satisfied to identify the conditions in terms of the marketplace. She noted that the marketplace conditions were defined by their own functions, components, and processes.

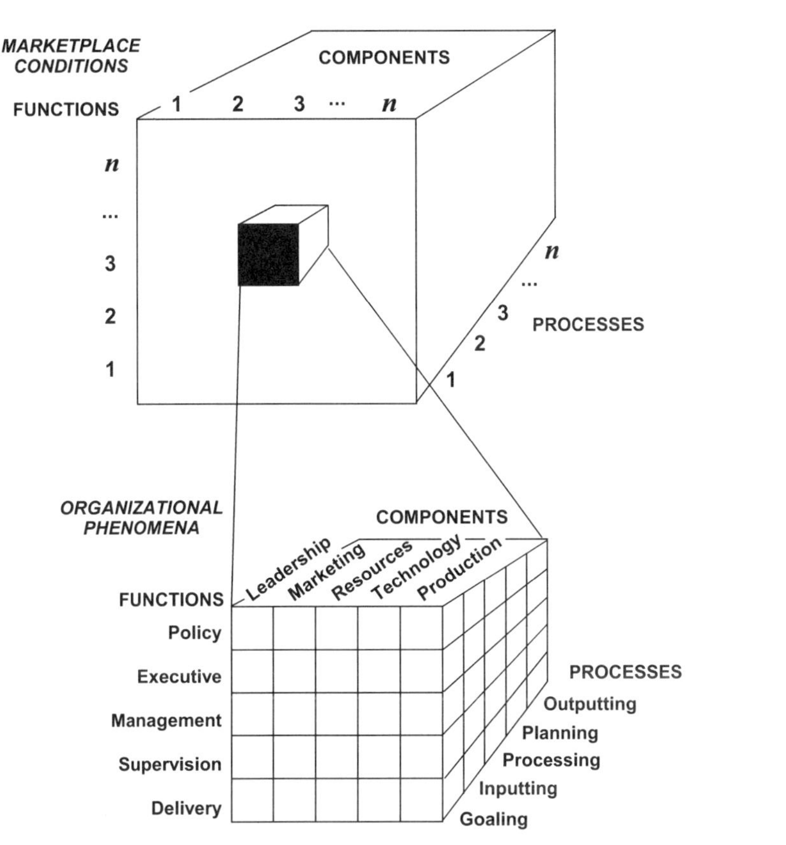

Figure 3-2. Organizational Phenomena and Marketplace Conditions

Next, Fisher needed to dimensionalize standards in order to culminate organizational operations (see Figure 3-3). She knew that organizational functioning could not be measured until standards had been assessed; however, she also knew that she was defining standards in a very different manner. She noted that the standards were drawn from the organizational units and defined in terms of human performance within the units. Consequently, as illustrated below, human standards were defined by leadership functions discharged by comprehensive human processing enabled by information modeling.

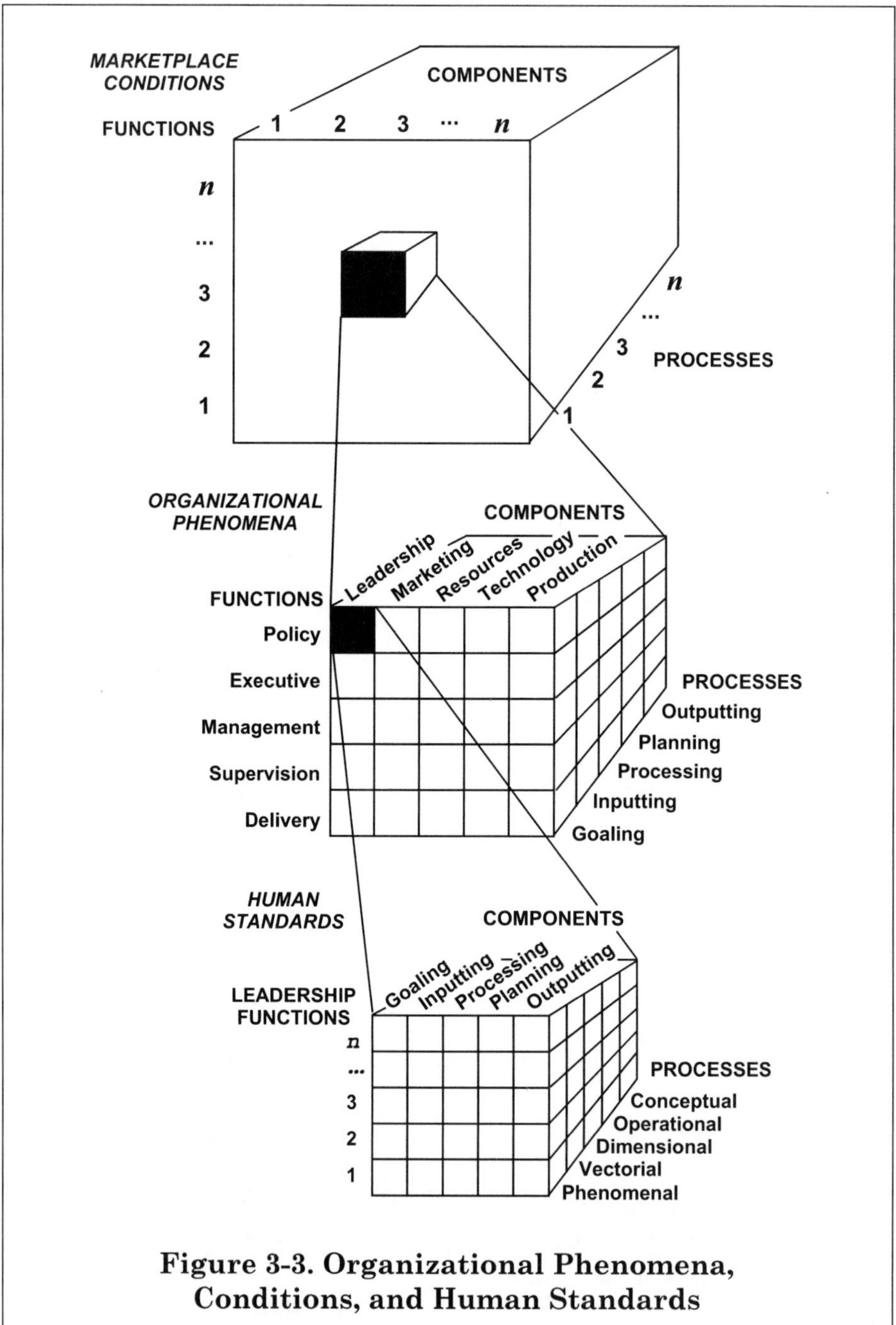

Figure 3-3. Organizational Phenomena, Conditions, and Human Standards

Fisher had completed her information-representing assignment by dimensionalizing all of the organizational operations. She understood the power of the marketplace conditions in generating organizational functions. She also recognized the critical nature of the interactions of organizational dimensions, and realized that the standards of human performance defined organizational effectiveness.

Our possibilities leader could now "see" the irony of the organizational system she was designing—that even as she dimensionalized organizational operations, the organization was assessing her standards of performance; that her performance would be assessed by human standards generated by organizational phenomena. She realized that the very process of dimensionalizing occurred within the policy cube: policy functions discharged by leadership components enabled by goaling processes. With great eagerness, Fisher began to recognize the full power of interdependent processing for developing a super-responsive, *"possibilities"* organization.

In summary, our possibilities leader now understood the power of dimensionalizing:

All phenomena have definable operations.

All phenomenal dimensions are interdependently related.

She was now prepared for individual processing.

INFORMATION REPRESENTING SYSTEMS

Possibilities management is, secondly, an information science. Information representing systems transform the raw data of experience into refined information. If empathizing with phenomena enables us to merge with phenomenal operations, then representing information dimensionalizes phenomena for us and brings them to life. We represent phenomena as a precondition to processing with them. We cannot process what we have not represented.

Information representing is the next stage in possibilities management. After relating to merge with phenomena, possibilities managers develop cognitive images of the phenomenon. The goal of information representing, then, is to produce dimensional images of phenomena; in other words, we transform operational images into dimensional images (see Figure 3-4). As shown below, the dimensional images are represented by three-dimensional models that ***"dimensionalize"*** the operations: functions, components, processes, conditions, standards. All of this is accomplished by our information representing, or I^2, systems.

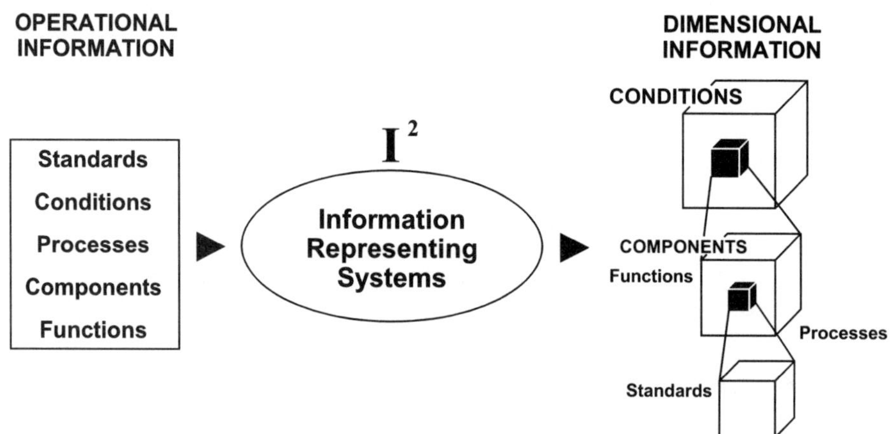

Figure 3-4. Information Representing Systems

Remember, it is not until we relate to merge with phenomena that we can define them operationally. Table 3-3 illustrates how operational information—with its levels of functions, components, processes, conditions, and standards—defines conceptual information.

Table 3-3. Operational Definitions of Conceptual Information

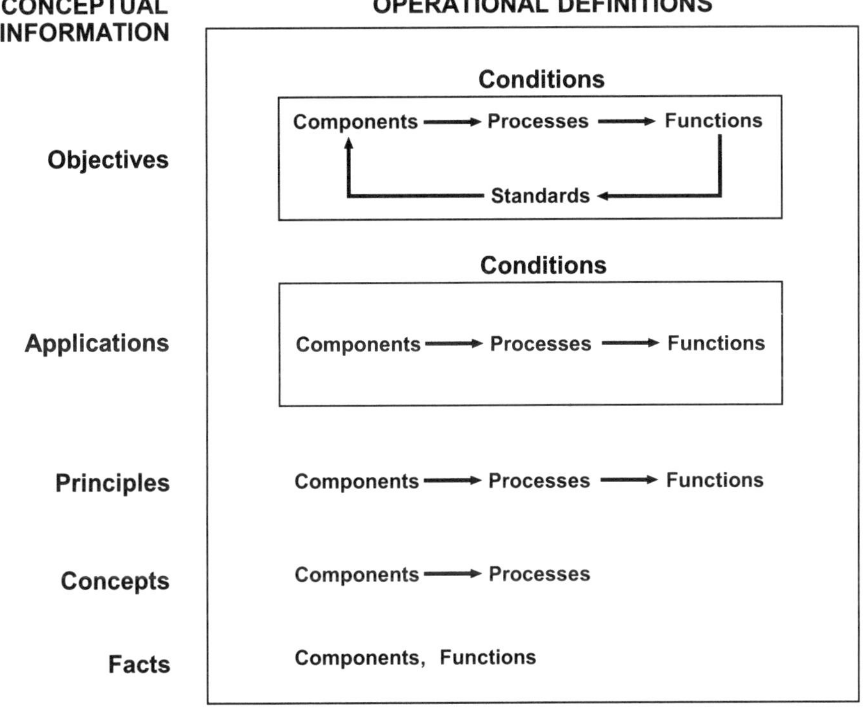

Relating to Operational Phenomena

The real test of relating for Terry was not in relating to people but to other entities. Relating to data operations was particularly difficult for him. *"How can I bring data to life?"* he asked himself. *"How can I relate to data as a tool of change?"* He resolved to use his relating skills to bring data to life.

Terry turned to data from a communication intervention he had introduced. He looked at the flat curve that assessed the effects of the intervention, and defined the curve operationally:

Components:	**The performance management systems**
Functions:	**failed to improve individual performance**
Processes:	**by increasing communication**
Conditions:	**under conditions of organizational productivity**
Standards:	**as measured by cost avoidance and other measures.**

Next, Terry related to his own experience:

RELATING SKILLS	SELF-RESPONSES
INITIATING (Operations)	"You are excited because you can now interpret the many operations imbedded in your data."
PERSONALIZING (Operations)	"You are disappointed because you cannot interpret the operations imbedded in your data."
RESPONDING (Operations)	"You are angry because your data don't tell you anything."
RESPONDING (Concepts)	"You are confused because you believed the data would be of value to you."
ATTENDING (Concepts)	"You are afraid that none of the data you produce makes a difference in management."

Terry continued to relate to the many operations imbedded in the data. He found many experiments *"nested"* within the data. He saw many performance curves for his human capital. They ranged from non-performance or default to exemplary performance. Since the management intervention was his initiative, he analyzed the *"non-results"* with great intensity.

A few of Terry's people did not perform at all. To be sure, they had resisted the project in the first place, criticized it in the second place, and performed dysfunctionally in the third place. Terry considered them *"detractors,"* and defined their operations accordingly:

> *Detractors make conditioned negative responses and perform dysfunctionally under conditions of organizational intervention with significant losses in productivity benefits.*

He now understood their mode of operating. Rather than condemning these *"detractors,"* he resolved to relate more intensely to merge with their experience of their performance.

Others among Terry's people had not even begun to participate in the project. To Terry, they seemed to be waiting and watching for how it would turn out. He considered them *"observers,"* and defined their operations as follows:

> *Observers continue to make their conditioned neutral responses and perform in their historic manner under conditions of organizational intervention with resulting flat curves in productivity.*

In some ways, Terry was most concerned about these *"observers"* because they entertained the failure as well as the success of the project. He resolved to relate to their modes of operating in the hope of enhancing their operations.

Terry found that most of his people participated at some minimal level, with a resulting minimal level of benefits. He considered these people *"participants,"* and defined their operations accordingly:

> *Participants make discriminative responses and perform in an incremental manner under conditions of organizational intervention with resulting minimal incremental growth in productivity.*

While evaluating their performance as satisfactory, Terry was concerned with these *"participants"* because they generated minimal benefits. He knew he had to relate to their experience in order to enable them to relate to the project's experience.

Increasingly, Terry realized that the performers to whom he would turn would be those who were to some degree successful. Some of his people had taken the project seriously and had modified their procedures to generate hundreds of thousands of dollars in *"cost-avoidance savings."* Terry labeled these people *"contributors,"* and defined their operations as follows:

> *Contributors make generative responses to perform in a growthful manner under conditions of organizational intervention with significant cost-avoidance benefits.*

For Terry, these contributors had performed as expected, and he was well pleased with their results. He did not know if greater productivity was possible, but resolved to find out by relating further.

It was not until Terry reviewed the results of one particular performer that he began to understand what was possible. This performer had taken the organizational intervention very seriously; he had actually generated productivity improvements worth millions of dollars by generating entirely new systems and, in at least one instance, new technologies to implement the systems. Terry labeled him *"a leader,"* and defined his operations as follows:

The leader employs generative processing to align with the intentions of the organization and, accordingly, emits exemplary performance with dramatic productivity benefits.

For Terry, the leader was the exemplar: the performer to emulate. Terry resolved to relate to the leader's experience for his own learning purposes.

By now, Terry had realized that performance was a *"continuing videotape,"* not a *"still photo."* Accordingly, to redefine and enhance the project's operations, he needed to relate not only to the performer's experiences but also to the project's experience. He started by interrelating all of the performers. Utilizing the leader as an exemplar, he defined minimal standards for performance one level above current performance.

The important discovery for Terry was that he could relate to data as a "lifeful" processing entity. By relating to merge with the intentionality of the intervention project, Terry could begin to see the variability and potential for changeability within the flat assessment curve. He had brought the data to life. He had transformed facts into operations. Moreover, he had initiated a new series of operations to enhance the organizational management intervention. He was on the verge of generating possibilities.

Terry summarized with an operational definition:

The objective of relating systems is to transform conceptual information into phenomenal information.

He liked to translate this definition in terms of basic interrogatives:

Who is doing *what? How* are they doing it? *Why, when, where,* and *how well* are they doing it?

Terry also summarized operational information in the formula *"5W2H,"* which represents the basic interrogatives: *who, what, why, when, where, how,* and *how well?* He noted that the 5Ws were made effective by the 2Hs.

Terry now prepared his own job aid for relating:

Relating skills generate operational information. The ARRPI relating skills include the following: attending, responding to concepts, responding to operations, personalizing, and initiating. The operational information is symbolized by *5W2H.*

The great learning for Terry was that relating brought phenomena to greater "lifefulness." By relating to generate operational information, he brought his own staff to life, his data to life, his organizational units to life. Indeed, he brought himself to life. To be sure, relating initiated generating. All generating, Terry concluded, begins with relating.

It is our dimensionalizing of operational information that prepares us for all meaningful processing. Operational information is linear. Dimensional information is multidimensional: it represents all levels of all dimensions in all of their various interactions. It is not until we have defined phenomena dimensionally that we can begin to process the phenomena. Dimensional information is a requirement for the twenty-first-century possibilities manager. Information representing, or modeling, is its source.

The Image Maker

Tom was determined to be *"the leader"* in Terry's management intervention project. He was manager of production. He had demonstrated greater productivity benefits than his management counterparts: he had designed new systems and technologies that generated exponentially more productivity improvement and cost-avoidance savings. He was the exemplar who could drive the entire organization, but only if elevated in his performance by an empowering intervention!

Because Tom had been involved with machines in engineering all of his life, he understood the limitations of other people's representations of their work assignments. He contrasted their representations with his nice, clean engineering systems: component inputs; procedures; function outputs. He labeled the others *"the image makers."*

Tom realized that people needed some way to represent their objectives or tasks schematically. He noted that almost all of the managers fell short of this standard. Not only did they communicate conceptually, but they seemed to approach their assignments conceptually. Even when they presented pictures, the pictures were random and idiosyncratic—never systematic. Even when they stated a relationship between entities, they never knew exactly how and why these entities were related. Tom concluded that their efforts to achieve their objectives were doomed. Indeed, these managers would never know whether they had achieved their objectives.

Tom acknowledged that some managers could define their objectives operationally. However, he found these managers to be linear, or one-dimensional, thinkers. They were fine when they had to design linear programs to achieve their operationally defined objectives. Some even designed parallel programs to achieve the objectives. But always, for Tom, the programs were one-dimensional: step-by-step programs to achieve the objectives.

Tom further acknowledged that a few managers had learned to think in two dimensions. They designed matrices to define objectives; they even developed two-dimensional branching systems to achieve those objectives. But Tom knew that, however much an improvement over the linear, two-dimensional representations had limitations. Neither nature nor man-made machines could be represented fruitfully in this manner.

Reinforced by his work in CAD-CAM, Tom prided himself in three-dimensional representations. Three-dimensional machine architecture drove three-dimensional manufacturing; it represented experimental improvement in performance and productivity. Yet even Tom had to admit there were limitations to the system. For one thing, it drove straight toward its objective: it was a production tool. For another, it had limited dimensionality: basically, it related components to components.

Tom realized that his three-dimensional representing was a tool for the planning paradigm. As such, it never could represent the full potential of any entity. Consequently, he never could systematically generate *"breakthroughs"* in his thinking. Tom recognized that he had to dedicate his three-dimensional expertise to multidimensional model-building in preparation for generative processing. He concluded that he was an *"image maker"* himself, and resolved to become an *information modeler*.

INFORMATION REPRESENTING SKILLS

In representing information at the highest levels, then, the possibilities manager represents the dimensionality of the phenomenon. In effect, the possibilities manager uses his or her *empathy* to accurately grasp the power and complexity of the phenomenon; then, the manager represents or models the phenomenon in some meaningful way. Although there are many levels of information representing systems, *dimensionalized information* is the most powerful and useful information representing system for possibilities managers. Dimensional information includes:

- **1D**—One-dimensional, linear information;
- **2D**—Two-dimensional, matrixed information;
- **3D**—Three-dimensional modeled information;
- **ND**—*Nested*-dimensional modeled information;
- **MD**—Multidimensional-*nested* modeled information.

We may view the systems of such information representing in the scale below (Table 3-4). This skills outline is presented developmentally, from 1D, 2D, 3D to *nested-D* (ND) and multidimensional (MD) information representation. Cumulatively, these skills enable us to represent dimensional images of any phenomena.

Table 3-4. Information Representing Systems

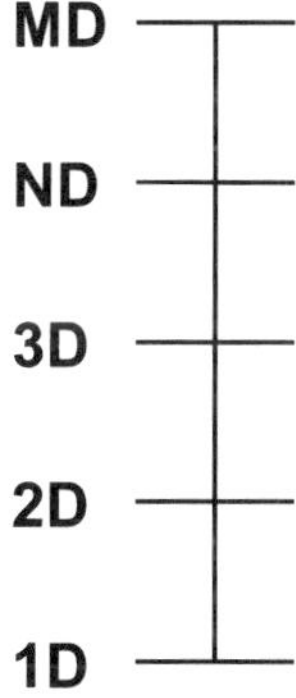

We may also view the Information Representing Matrix in Table 3-5. As may be noted, the information-relating functions are rotated to become components dedicated to information-representing functions. We may summarize the objective of information representing as follows:

> *Information-relating components (I^1) are dedicated to discharging information-representing functions (I^2).*

In other words, we relate to merge with phenomena so that we can represent images of the phenomena.

Table 3-5. Information Representing Matrix

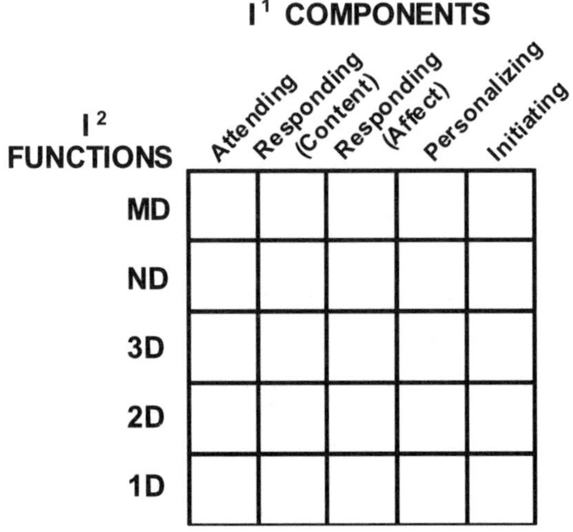

One-Dimensional Information

The most basic mode of representing information is the one-dimensional mode (see Table 3-6). This linearity is illustrated as an x axis. By way of example, the components of phenomena could be represented in a linear scale.

Table 3-6. One-Dimensional Information

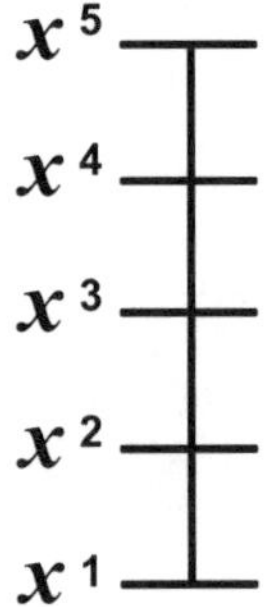

One-dimensional information is a commonly used form of information representation and so quite recognizable. The simplest example of such information would be a list. Of course, organizing systems such as "set theory" make linear listing useful. Unfortunately, we have all been presented with poorly organized lists that lack any discernable "set theory" construction. A well-organized list continues to be a basic, useful output of information representation. The value of one-dimensional information is determined by the quality of the information-organizing systems we apply—how we organize our "sets" of information.

Possibilities managers may maximize their application of one-dimensional information modeling by applying and empowering the use of 1D information-building skills. The use of nominal, ordinal, interval, and process scaling elevates the power of one-dimensional information representations and brings new functionality to this level of information.

Table 3-7 provides an example of a one-dimensional representation of information. Here, the information simply conveys an organization's functional levels: policy, executive, management, supervision, and delivery.

Table 3-7. One-Dimensional Representation of Organizations

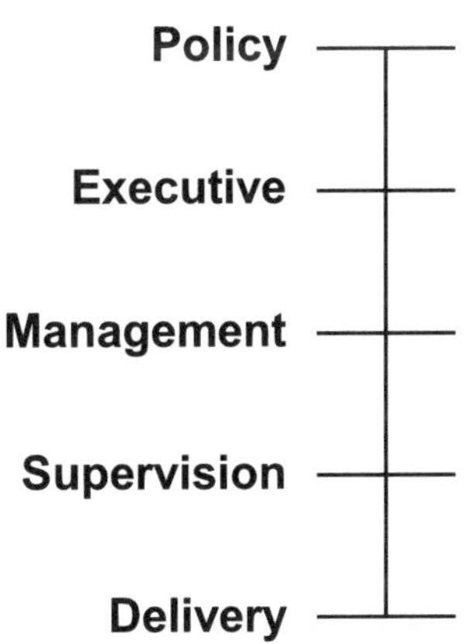

Two-Dimensional Information

At the next level, information is represented by a two-dimensional matrixed image. In Table 3-8, this is depicted by the intersection of ***x*** and ***y*** axes in the upper-left window. The scaled components and functions of phenomena are represented in the two-dimensional, interactional matrix shown on the right.

Table 3-8. Two-Dimensional Information

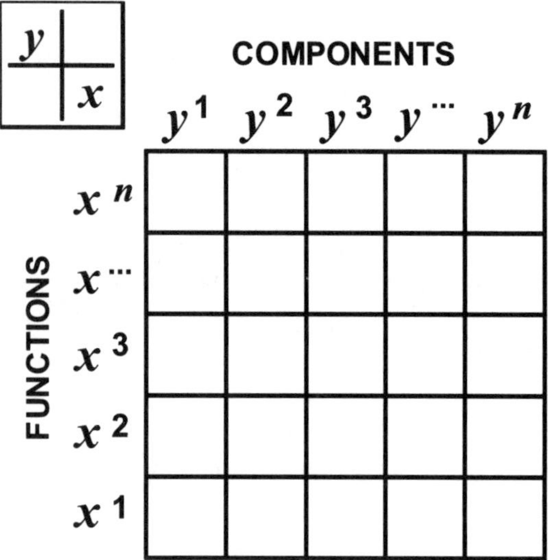

Two-dimensional information is also a commonly used and recognizable form of information representation. The simplest expressions involve matrices (or tables) and graphs. Our methods for organizing information determine which information we choose to represent along each axis. Spreadsheets are common two-dimensional information representations. Computer databases structure linear information as files or lists and store matrices as tables. We can build our own matrices (or tables) as we want or need them. The keys to representing productive two-dimensional information, however, are our cognitive systems for determining which information ingredients we choose to relate.

Possibilities managers may maximize their application of two-dimensional information modeling by applying and empowering the use of 2D information-building skills. For example, by bringing into interaction a combination of nominal, ordinal, interval, and process scales, we can reveal new information and insights.

Table 3-9 illustrates a two-dimensional representation of organizations. This matrix adds the organizational components of leadership, marketing, resources, technology, and production.

Table 3-9. Two-Dimensional Representation of Organizations

FUNCTIONS \ COMPONENTS	Leadership	Marketing	Resources	Technology	Production
Policy					
Executive					
Management					
Supervision					
Delivery					

Three-Dimensional Information

At the next level, we may view a three-dimensional model for representing information (see Figure 3-5). This dimensionality is depicted below by the convergence of ***x, y,*** and ***z*** axes in the upper-left window. In the illustration, the scaled components, functions, and processes are represented in a three-dimensional interactional model.

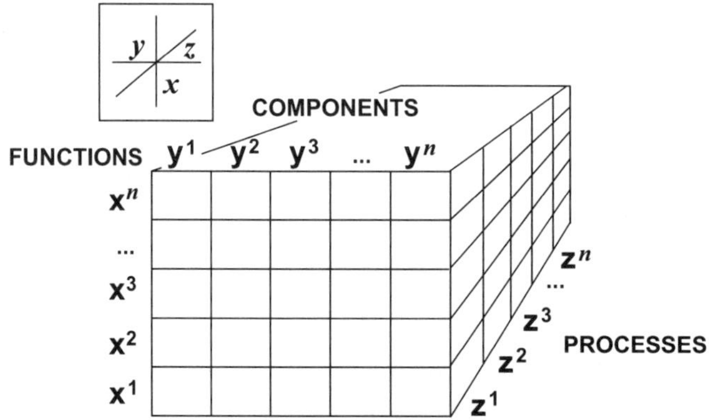

Figure 3-5. Three-Dimensional Information

Three-dimensional information is a much less commonly used form of information representation. Yet, 3D information is powerful in its utility.

Possibilities managers may maximize their application of three-dimensional information modeling by introducing 3D information-building skills. The interaction of multiple types of scales brings new functionality to three-dimensional information.

Figure 3-6 presents a three-dimensional representation of organizations. As shown, this model adds the organizational processes of goaling, inputting, processing, planning, and outputting.

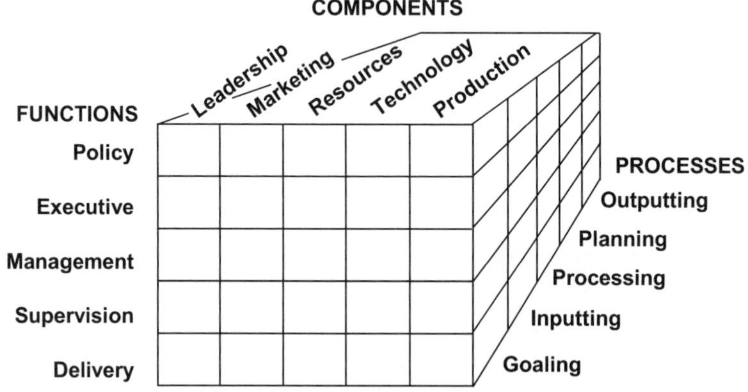

Figure 3-6. Three-Dimensional Representation of Organizations

In our organizations, people will not be fully empowered until they can represent information in three dimensions. Now, for the first time, they can understand the critical interactions of multiple levels of all dimensions. For the first time, they can extract a cell or a cube of information and concentrate upon the interaction of these converged dimensions.

"Nested"-Dimensional Information

We can represent more complex information by *"nesting"* our models in other higher-order models (see Figure 3-7). This means introducing new axes or planes within which to *house* our models. These axes represent the relationships between additional phenomenal dimensions. In our illustration, the scaled components, functions, and processes are represented as a *nested* three-dimensional interactional model.

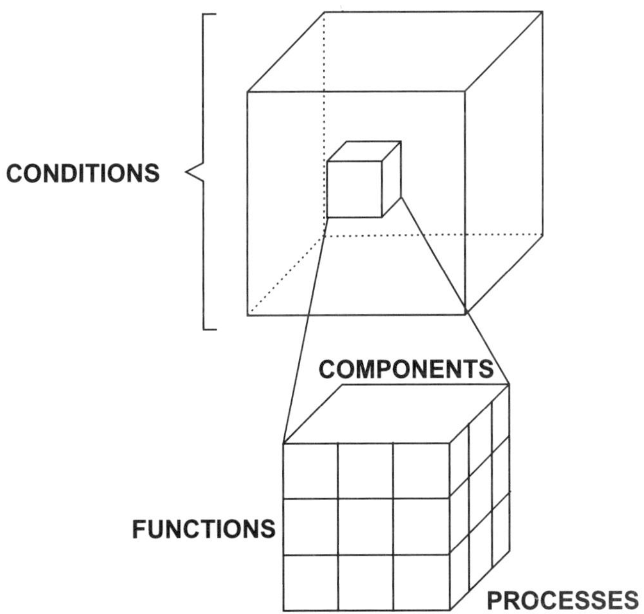

Figure 3-7. *Nested*-Dimensional Information

With *nested*-dimensional information, powerful new information is revealed. *Nested* information delivers the conditions in which phenomena function, and so delivers invaluable perspective.

Possibilities managers may maximize their application of *nested*-dimensional information modeling by introducing skills in *nested*-dimensional information. The interaction of multiple 3D models delivers new, functional information.

Figure 3-8 illustrates a representation of an organization *nested* in the marketplace. As we can see, the organization is positioned in one cube of the marketplace, or one market space. In this instance, this means the organization is *nested* in the market space of information technology (IT) providers servicing human capital development (HCD) market requirements and employing technological organization processes.

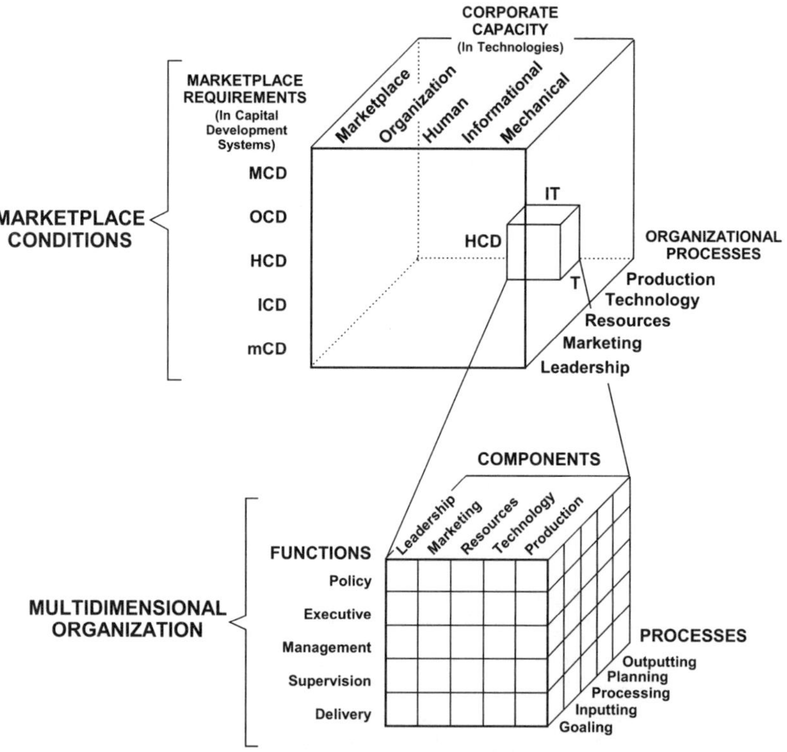

Figure 3-8. *Nested* Representation of Organizations

In our organizations, people will not really have perspective until they understand the *"nesting"* of one model within another. This is especially true for understanding the full assumptions and implications of the conditions within which we operate. It is also true for the assumptions and implications of the conditions for entities of any kind: organizations in the marketplace; units within organizations; humans within units; information within humans; mechanical tools in service of fulfilling information designs.

Multidimensional Information

The most advanced mode of representing information is the multidimensional mode. An example of multidimensional information is shown in Figure 3-9. Multidimensional information simply adds information by introducing new axes or planes.

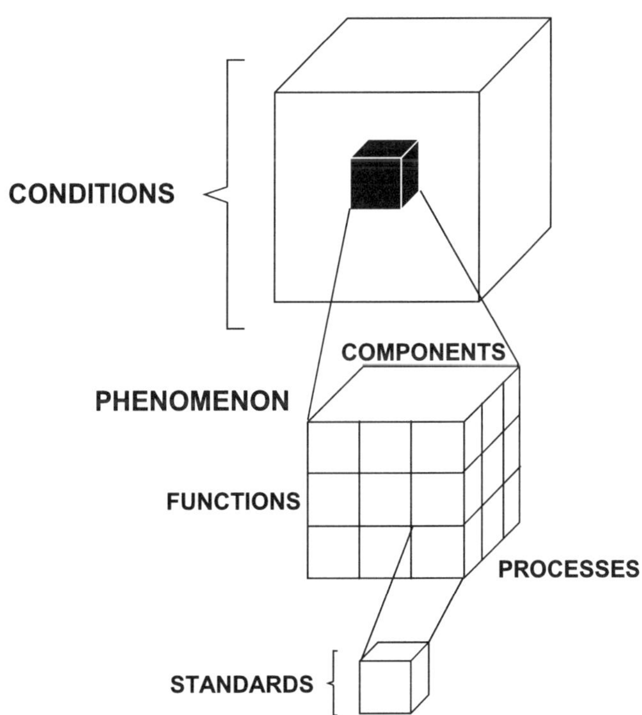

Figure 3-9. Multidimensional Information

We continue to represent multidimensional systems in a three-dimensional manner. As may be noted, the 3D models are *nested* in higher-order models that represent conditions; in turn, they *nest* lower-order models that represent standards. *All models of higher- and lower-order phenomena have their own dimensionality: functions, components, processes.*

With multidimensional information, powerful new information is revealed. Multidimensional information includes the standards for measuring how the phenomena perform as well as the conditions in which the phenomena function. This multidimensional information lends invaluable perspective.

Possibilities managers may maximize their application of multidimensional information modeling by introducing skills in information-building at the multidimensional level. The interaction of multiple 3D models delivers new, functional information.

To represent our organization multidimensionally, we begin by representing our organization in three dimensions (see Figure 3-10). Next, we represent the organization's conditions by presenting a visual image of where our organization is *nested* within a marketplace model. Finally, we represent the standards of human performance for each or any unit of the organization.

We may now summarize a dimensional definition of the phenomenon:

> *Organizational functions are discharged by organizational components enabled by organizational processes under marketplace conditions at standards of human performance.*

We now know everything we need to know about the phenomenon in order to process it.

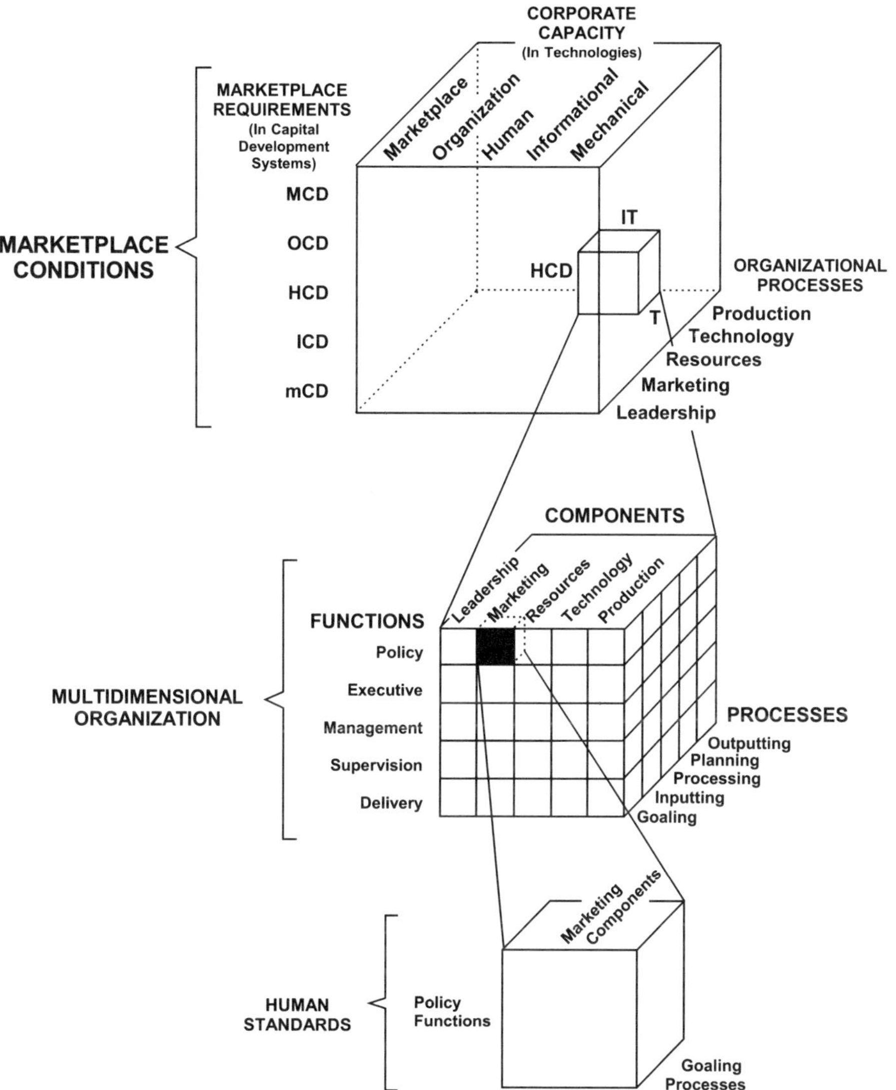

Figure 3-10. Multidimensional Representation of Organizations

The Information Modeler

As the exemplary performer in the performance management system, Tom was charged with designing the new productivity improvement system. Realizing that he needed to be more than just an *image maker,* he pursued training in information representing. Once that training was completed, Tom was able to consider himself an *information modeler.* He believed that he could model the experiences of any phenomena—whether people, data, or things. From his new perspective, he could fully see the limitations of his former three-dimensional representations. Here is what Tom now knew.

First, his earlier representations did not include all of the operations of an entity, or phenomenon. Most of the time, they simply related one set of components to other sets of components to achieve objectives. They never related all of the operations:

Functions, Components, Processes, Conditions, Standards

Second, systematic interdependent modeling is a genuine discipline, and must be learned. All individual dimensions are scaled and all dimensions are related cumulatively and interactively to all of the other dimensions:

Functions x Components x Processes x Conditions x Standards

Third, multidimensional modeling is rigorous. All multidimensional models are related to other multidimensional models: the multidimensional phenomena under focus are *nested* in phenomenal conditions that are themselves multidimensional models; the multidimensional phenomena also generate *nested* phenomenal standards that are themselves multidimensional models. These relationships may be expressed as:

Most important, through training Tom came to understand the meaning of the relationships between dimensions. For the first time, he truly understood, in engineering terms, the meaning of phenomenal conditions. Everything comes from something! Tom began to comprehend the following:

- How people working at individual workstations usually operate within unit- or organization-wide conditions, which, in turn, operate within the marketplace.
- How the organizational components, which drive on marketplace functions, generate the functions for human capital operating within the units;
- How the human processing components, which drive our organizational functions, generate the functions for information-capital standards.

Tom was now able to appreciate how his engineering work was part of an integrated whole, and got to work on applying what he had learned.

Productivity Improvement

Tom began his productivity-improvement work by considering productive organizational potential, or **POP.** He saw POP in terms of individual performance-improvement programs, or **PIP.**

$$\underline{\text{POP}} = f(\underline{\text{PIP}})$$

In this formula, productivity improvement is a function of the cumulative and interactive effects of individual performance improvement.

Accordingly, Tom represented his *nested* models for PIP within the organizational conditions of POP:

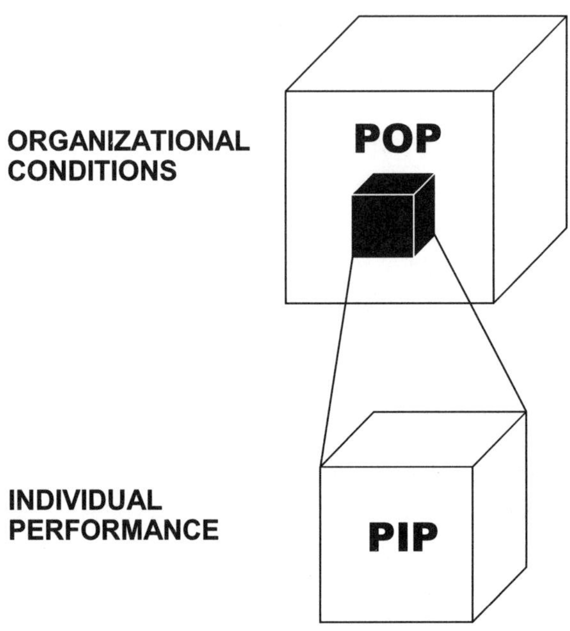

Next, Tom began to develop images of the performance improvement programs, or PIP. He viewed himself and his colleagues as human resources. He defined the resources physically, emotionally, and intellectually and multiplied them (P • E • I) in the formula for performance improvement:

$$\underline{\mathbf{PIP}} = \mathbf{P \cdot E \cdot I}$$

In this formula, performance improvement is a function of the multiplication of physical, emotional, and intellectual resources required for task performance.

Tom represented this basic model multidimensionally:

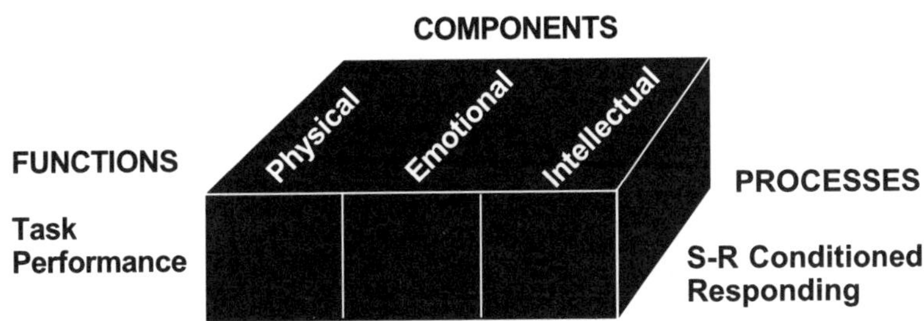

He defined his PIP model operationally:

> *Functional tasks are discharged by physical, emotional, and intellectual resource components enabled by S-R conditioned responding processes.*

The physical resources emphasized the physical fitness necessary to perform the tasks. The emotional resources emphasized the motivation necessary to perform the tasks. The intellectual resources emphasized the information relating skills necessary to define the operations needed to perform the tasks. Tom realized that these were the minimum resources required to perform basic tasks.

Tom also realized that managers needed to be able to achieve these operationally defined objectives. Accordingly, he elevated the power of the emotional and intellectual resources in the following formula:

$$\underline{PIP} = P \cdot E^2 \cdot I^2$$

In this formula, performance improvement programs are a function of exponential multiplication; emotional resources are expanded to incorporate interpersonal skills; intellectual resources are elevated to include information representation systems.

Tom represented this advanced PIP model multidimensionally:

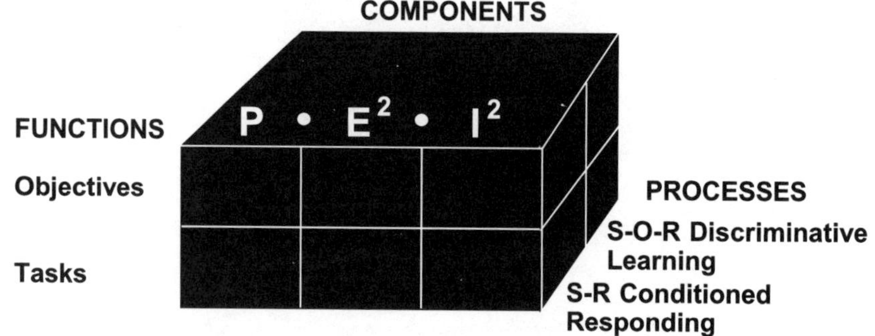

He defined this elevated PIP model operationally:

> *Functional objectives are discharged by emphasizing exponentially multiplied emotional and intellectual resources enabled by S-O-R discriminative learning processes.*

Tom culminated the model by incorporating the management need to be able to design systems. Accordingly, he further elevated the power of the intellectual resources as follows:

$$\underline{\mathbf{PIP}} = \mathbf{P \cdot E^2 \cdot I^3}$$

In this formula, performance improvement programs are functions of further exponential multiplication; the intellectual resources are elevated to incorporate generative processing.

Tom represented this culminating PIP model multidimensionally:

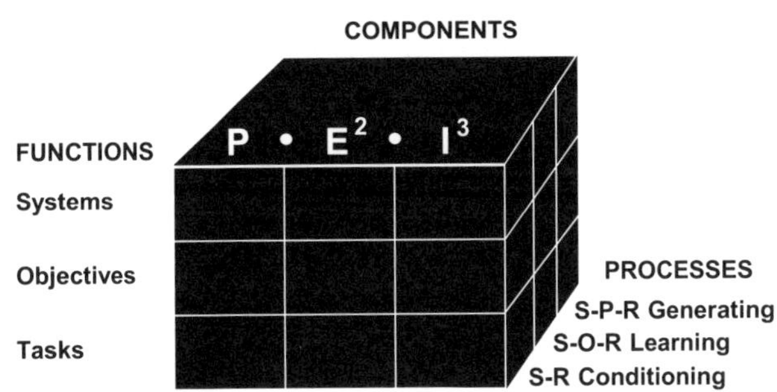

He also defined this culminating PIP model operationally:

> *Functional systems designs are discharged by emphasizing exponentially multiplied intellectual resources enabled by S-P-R processing.*

Tom represented the developmental stations in his PIP. He labeled them in human resource terms:

- *Human Resources (HR)*—the physical, emotional, and intellectual resources necessary to perform basic day-to-day tasks (T);
- *Human Resource Development (HRD)*—the resources, especially emotional-interpersonal and intellectual-informational, needed to achieve operational objectives (O);
- *Human Capital Development (HCD)*—the resources, especially intellectual and generative, necessary to design systems (S).

He concluded that all managers must be empowered to become human capital.

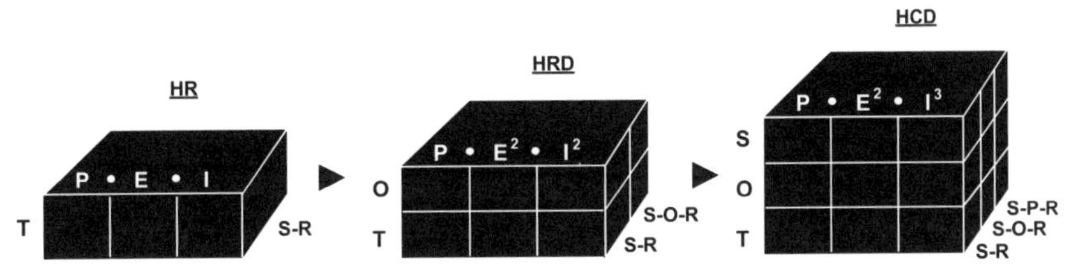

Just as Tom had represented the organizational conditions from which the HCD requirements were derived, he now represented the standards by which human performance would be measured. As may be noted, these standards are information standards; thus, we will measure HCD by information capital development, or ICD. *"Just take a look at the management system that I have designed for HCD,"* Tom pointed out. *"It is a prima facie case for information modeling for ICD!"* He noted that HCD and ICD were synergistically related: each produced elevated levels of the other.

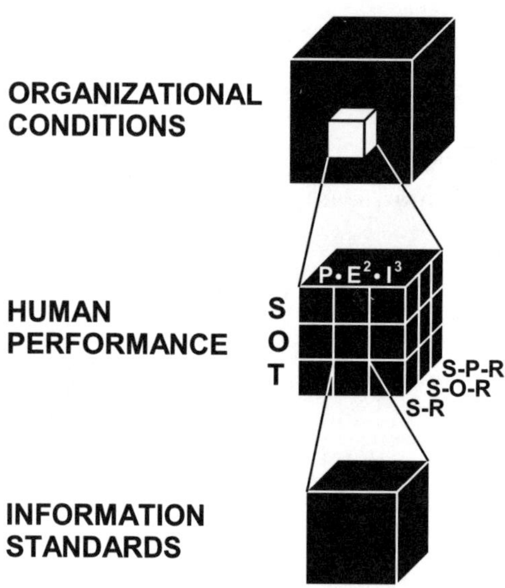

Tom recognized that there was a great deal more to be learned. He was satisfied with his effort only as a beginning phase. He understood that the human capital standards in the twenty-first century would be spiraling ones. His research led him to project that his next several stations would lead to prime HCD:

$$\underline{\mathbf{HCD}}' = \mathbf{f(P \cdot E^2 \cdot I^5)}$$

He understood further that this would generate escalating levels of PIP and POP. The actualization of these performance and productivity functions became the enduring mission in his life.

Above all else, Tom resolved that he would become the exemplary performer who drives organizational productivity as well as production. He had become an *information modeler,* and now he would become a *human model* as well. He defined his new leadership role in operation terms:

> *The exemplar models elevated performance by generative human processing to improve organizational productivity with measurable standards of powerful and changing, interdependent multidimensional models.*

It remained for Tom to conquer the human processing systems for which information representing had prepared him.

In Transition

The threshold skill of informational representing is 3D modeling. Once we have modeled phenomena in three dimensions, we can dimensionalize phenomena comprehensively. Three-D modeling means that we fully represent our understanding of the dimensions of the phenomena: components, functions, processes. In addition, we represent our understanding of the interactions of all levels of each dimension. Moreover, we can go on to represent the conditions of the phenomena and their standards.

In terms of managing the representation of information as part of daily tasks, it is critical that we emphasize dimensionalized representations of tasks. *Concepts* are inadequate and lead to confusion. *Operational information* is useful, but is limited in its comprehensiveness. Only *dimensionalized representations* model phenomena comprehensively. They tell all of us about the robust multidimensionality of the phenomena.

A valuable tool for managing I^2 is presented in Table 3-10. With this tool, we may assess our employees' levels of functioning in representing phenomena:

1. Can our employees represent the phenomena with a linear (1D) scale of any dimension?
2. Can they represent the phenomena's functions and components in a 2D matrix?
3. Can they represent the phenomena's functions, components, and processes in a 3D model?
4. Can they represent the phenomenal conditions in *nested*-dimensional (ND) modeling?
5. Can they represent the phenomenal conditions and standards in multidimensional (MD) modeling?

Table 3-10. I^2 Management Systems

	AREAS OF PHENOMENA		
LEVELS OF I^2	**People**	**Data**	**Things**
MD			
ND			
3D			
2D			
1D			

The answers to these questions will dictate our level of confidence in our employees and their representations.

Case: The Possibilities Leader (continued)

As we have seen, our possibilities leader, Sharon Fisher, was now ready to go on to individual processing. Through her experience in the representing phase, she had learned the truth of the following:

- *All things can be processed once they are represented dimensionally.* Without dimensional information, there can be no systematic processing; with it, there are potentially infinite possibilities. Dimensionally represented information introduces managers and phenomena to each other's dimensional possibilities.
- *Information representing is not only a skill, but also an attitude:* an attitude of respect, commitment, and perseverance. Respect for the complexity of phenomena! Commitment to actualizing phenomenal potential! Perseverance in working toward the growth of both manager and phenomena!

  Multidimensional information modeling communicates this respect because the multidimensional emphasizes interdependency. It is the interdependent processing of multidimensional systems that yields growth for all parties. Accuracy in information representing is a critical requirement for the possibilities manager in the twenty-first-century global marketplace.

In addition, Fisher had begun to comprehend her own power in generating standards for measuring the excellence of her own performance. She understood that, as human capital, she was *nested* within the multidimensional conditions of her organization, and that she herself constituted the conditions for the standards of her people's performance.

In short, bits of data are transformed into dimensionalized information: one-dimensional, two-dimensional, three-dimensional, *nested*-dimensional, and multidimensional (see Figure 3-11). By representing information dimensionally, we elevate our level of interrelating to merge with phenomena. In turn, elevated sensitive and empathic relating facilitates our understanding of the complexity and power of the phenomena. In this way, information representing prepares us for individual processing, or thinking: the skills to process the information that we have represented.

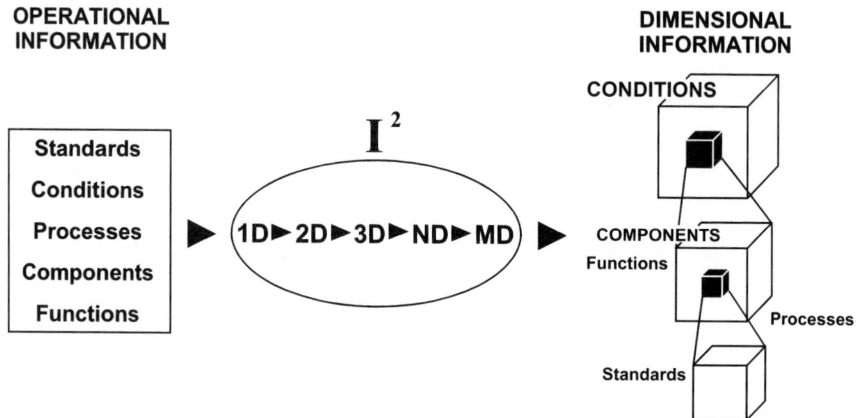

Figure 3-11. Information Representing Systems

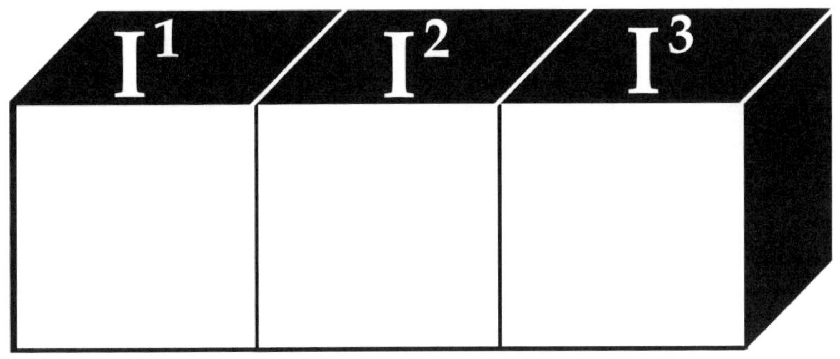

4 I^3—Individual Processing Systems

Individual processing is the source of phenomenal generativity.

Information modeling enables us to process generatively. Generative processing empowers us to create new responses that the stimuli were not intended to elicit. In other words, we break the bonds of conditioned responding. We do so by inserting the multidimensional models within our processing. These models empower us to expand a multitude of options that we could not see in our linear processing. The expanded options allow us to narrow our choices of preferred alternatives based upon our personal or corporate values.

Case: The Possibilities Leader

— I^3 *Individual Processing*

Empowered by her perspective of dimensional models of conditions, Sharon Fisher was now prepared to process generatively. She began by establishing organizational goals, in this case, the corporate mission (see Figure 4-1). She defined the mission as follows:

- Public-sector targets,
- Consulting- and training-service goals,
- Leadership-driven organizational strategies.

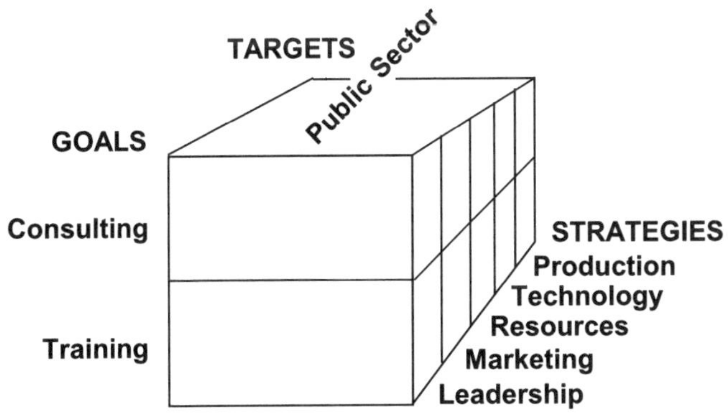

Figure 4-1. The Corporate Mission

She then summarized the mission in this operational definition:

> *Consulting- and training-service goals are accomplished with public-sector targets by way of leadership-driven organizational strategies.*

Next, Fisher analyzed the current operations in terms of their ability to fill the super-responsive corporate mission (see Figure 4-2). She broke the operations down as follows:

> *Components inputs are transformed into functions outputs by processing.*

Fisher assessed the standards and discovered that the current inputs were ineffective and inefficient in accomplishing the outputs under the current conditions. She decided to expand alternative operations.

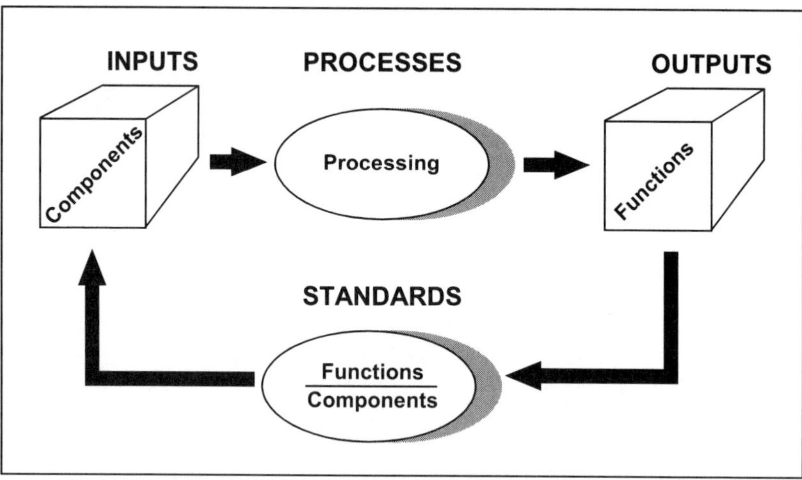

Figure 4-2. Analyzing the Current Corporation

Fisher drew her images of alternative models from information representing systems (see Figure 4-3). She expanded her alternatives by considering all functions, components, and processes in these systems. The combinations and permutations of the dimensions at all of these levels would enable her to synthesize new organizational models to meet her corporate mission.

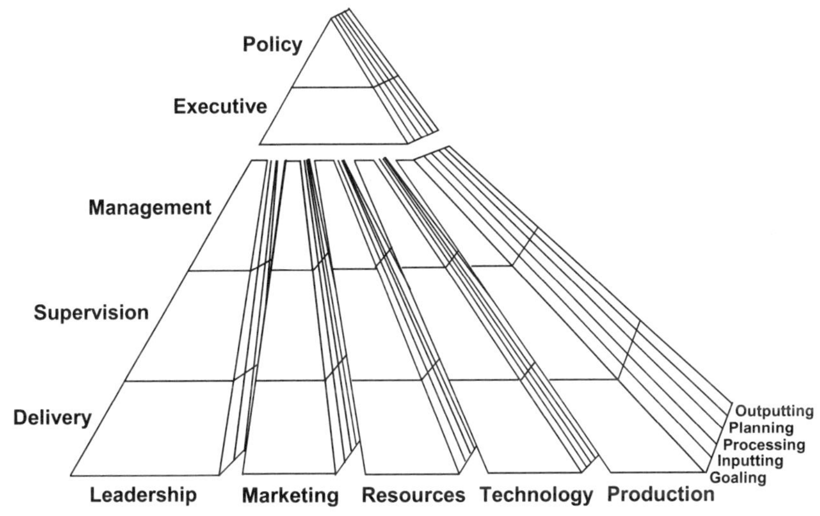

Figure 4-3. Synthesizing New Models

The illustration below (Figure 4-4) shows how Fisher operationalized her newly synthesized model. As may be noted, her organizational model is centralized by mission and decentralized by operations. In this image, the policy and executive levels have the responsibility for leading and "architecting" the organization. In turn, the marketing, resource integration, technology, and production operations are decentralized. This decentralized design manages the information problem and moves the corporation toward becoming super-responsive to the marketplace.

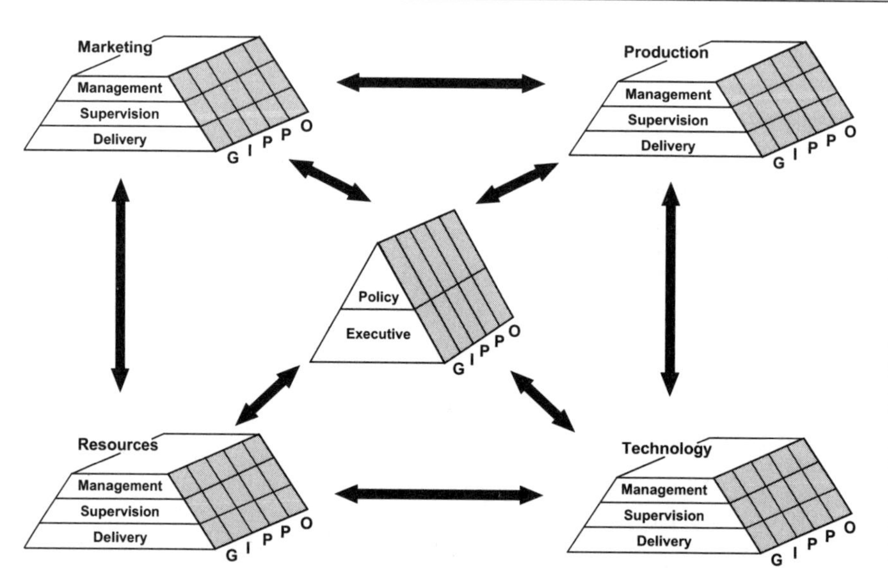

Figure 4-4. Operationalizing New Models

In technologizing the new model, Fisher found (among many nuances) that teams were more productive than formal hierarchical levels (see Figure 4-5). Accordingly, she designed management-led, team-based operations, thereby eliminating one level of hierarchy. With input and feedback from the people involved, she designed an increasingly flexible and responsive stroking force, thereby further alleviating the oppressive effects of the monolithic organization.

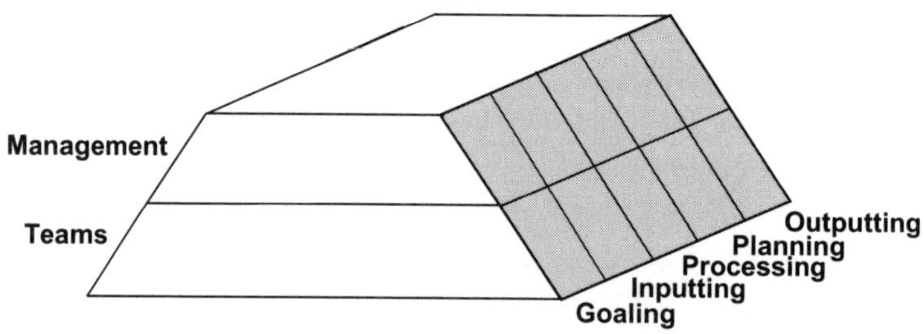

Figure 4-5. Technologizing the New Model

Our possibilities leader was now approaching completion of her assignment. Because of her individual processing skills, she already had an early image of a super-responsive organizational model, one that included:

- I^1 *Operational phenomena,*
- I^2 *Dimensional phenomena,*
- I^3 *Generative phenomena.*

It remained for her to engage others in interpersonal processing to generate the most powerful images of super-responsiveness.

INDIVIDUAL PROCESSING SYSTEMS

Possibilities management is, thirdly, a generative processing science. *"Processing"* means transforming stimulus inputs into response outputs. *"Generative processing"* means transforming stimulus inputs into response outputs that the stimuli were not intended to elicit! The processor thus generates *new responses.* In so doing, the processor generates a *new stimulus environment* as well!

The goal of individual processing systems is to generate tailored images of the phenomena; in other words, we transform the dimensional images into phenomenal images (see Figure 4-6). Note that the phenomenal images are represented by tailored images that define the entities and their relationships in a *"virtual organization."* All of this is accomplished by our individual processing, or I^4, systems.

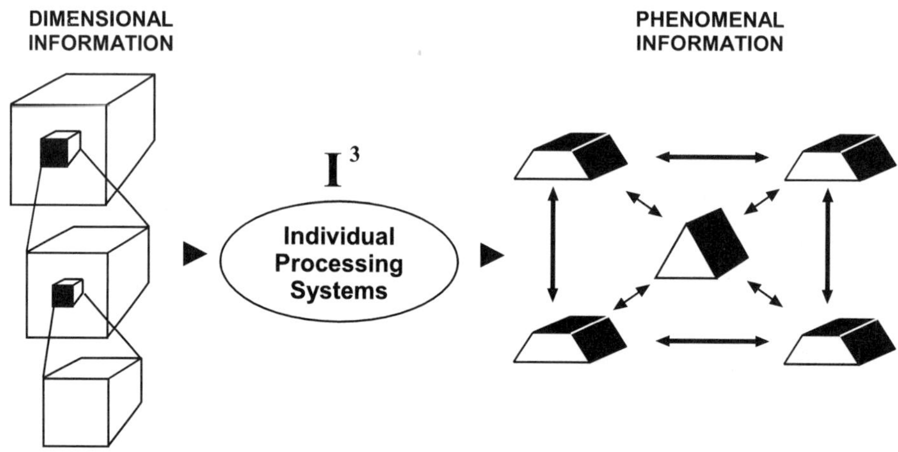

Figure 4-6. Individual Processing Systems

Individual processing is *possibilities thinking*. Possibilities thinkers begin by goaling systematically. The operative term here is "systematically"! They analyze their clients' current operations: Did the operations achieve their goals? If not, the thinkers synthesize images of more productive operations, initially expanding alternatives and then narrowing those alternatives to preferred courses. They rapidly prototype operational images. They technologize the solutions by developing programmatic steps to achieve those solutions. In short, the possibilities thinkers begin with the current operations of their clients and culminate the process in new and more productive operations.

Let us put individual processing into the perspective of the learning sciences. Almost everything we learn is ultimately incorporated as conditioned responses. Once we incorporate the conditioned responses we have learned, no real processing occurs between the stimulus input and the conditioned response. We are simply conditioned to make reflex responses.

Currently, management is dominated by participative thinkers, or discriminative learners. Armed with repertoires of conditioned responses, they make discriminations with their elaborate branching systems. However, no matter how elaborate, when those branching discriminations are reduced, they amount to only a hierarchy of conditioned responses. As processors, then, participative thinkers are highly limited.

The only truly productive processors are the *generative processors*. Armed with repertoires of discriminative processes, they generate entirely new and powerful responses. Moreover, they increasingly dedicate their generative processes toward acquiring more powerful processing systems.

The Discriminative Learners

Jesse was the head of the engineering group in Tom's production component. As such, he was familiar with Tom's mission: to improve organizational productivity by improving individual performance.

$$\underline{\mathbf{POP}} = \mathbf{f}(\underline{\mathbf{PIP}})$$

As we saw earlier, this formula means that productive organizational potential (POP) is a function of performance improvement programs (PIP).

Further, Jesse understood PIP to be a function of human capital development:

$$\underline{\mathbf{PIP}} = \mathbf{f}(\underline{\mathbf{HCD}})$$

This means that performance improvement programs are a function of HCD.

Finally, Jesse understood HCD to be a function of physical, emotional, and intellectual resource development:

$$\underline{\mathbf{HCD}} = \mathbf{f}(\mathbf{P} \cdot \mathbf{E}^2 \cdot \mathbf{I}^3)$$

Indeed, HCD is a function of physical, emotional, and intellectual resources. The intellectual resources are prepotent because of their systems:

- I^1—Information relating systems,
- I^2—Information representing systems,
- I^3—Individual processing systems.

Jesse had a special interest in the intellectual resources and their empowering processing systems.

In this regard, Jesse was quite proud of his group's track record: its output had grown appreciably every year for the last several years. However, his budget was now "frozen"; because of the spiraling changes in marketplace conditions, his group was being asked to do more with less. These issues were not far from Jesse's mind when Tom sat down with him to model the engineering group's role in manufacturing.

The two began by defining the engineering group's operations. Soon they agreed on this definition:

> *The engineering group "architects" the designs that drive production under increasingly market-centered conditions and human-centered standards.*

Both Tom and Jesse were aware of the following:

- Market-centered conditions revolve around the spiraling changes in the marketplace; they emphasize not only the historic cost-to-market but also the futuristic time-to-market.

- Human-centered standards revolve around human processing and human performance; they emphasize not only the historic consensus building but also the futuristic generative human processing.

In this context, then, how would the engineering group "architect" the manufacturing designs? According to Jesse, the group would engage in a consensus-building process:

1. They would formulate their goals for manufacturing.
2. They would then analyze their current operating procedures for achieving their goals.
3. If dissatisfied with their current operations, they would select *"best practices"* from the industry.

Tom voiced his concern about this approach: *"But how can we respond to market changes with 'best practices' and still differentiate our products and services in the marketplace?"*

Jesse reflected on what Tom had said. Then the light struck: *"You mean that 'best practices' will only put us back with pack!"*

The response was *"Yes. Work on it!"*

Jesse thought *long* and *hard* about it. He also thought *smart* about it by soliciting other people's advice, both within the group and without. There was no easy answer, no *"best practice"* antidote to the *"best practice"* problem. Jesse looked again at the definition of the engineering group's operations. He scrutinized the phase *"and human-centered standards."* He understood the consensus-building part: it was the signature of his generation. But he did not really understand the "generative human processing" part: it seemed to make no sense—or did it make a lot of sense? *"This must be the key!"* Jesse thought excitedly. *"The key to generating the breakthroughs and innovations that enable us to differentiate ourselves in the marketplace!"*

Without delay, Jesse put together an image of his engineers' current form of processing. He knew this processing was called *"discriminative learning."* We may also call it *"discriminative processing."*

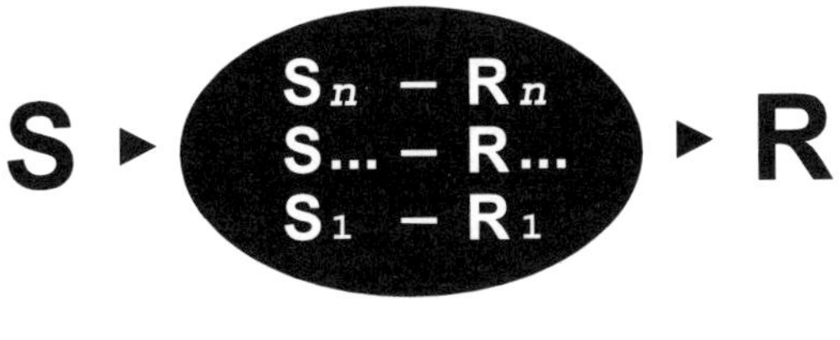

$$S \blacktriangleright \begin{pmatrix} S_n - R_n \\ S_{\dots} - R_{\dots} \\ S_1 - R_1 \end{pmatrix} \blacktriangleright R$$

He translated the image in this way: basically, the human organism is a repository of a hierarchy of conditioned responses (S-R); upon the presentation of the stimulus (S), the organism (O) discriminates its dimensions and then selects and emits the appropriate response (R) pattern to match the stimulus.

"What's wrong with that?" Jesse mused. *"Nothing,"* he answered himself, *"except it doesn't match the changing stimuli in the marketplace."* All of the following made good sense to him:

1. The effectiveness of discriminative processing requires a stable marketplace, one that gives us time to train and build response repertoires.
2. Our current marketplace is changing so rapidly that by the time we have trained people in the responses, those responses are no longer appropriate to the stimuli.
3. Spiraling change requires generative processing systems that empower the processor to generate entirely new responses and, indeed, generate their own new stimulus environments.

"What we need," Jesse concluded, *"is not 'best practices' to catch up with everybody else. What we need is 'best processes' for generating our own innovations!"*

Jesse was determined to discover them.

INDIVIDUAL PROCESSING SKILLS

In individual processing, or thinking, the possibilities manager processes the phenomena. This means that the manager has merged with the phenomena and represented them. For managers to process in this way, they must apply the generative processing systems scaled in Table 4-1 and detailed below.

- ***Goaling*** by measuring values;
- ***Analyzing*** by dissembling entities;
- ***Synthesizing*** by assembling new entities;
- ***Operationalizing*** by prototyping new entities;
- ***Technologizing*** by producing the new entities.

Table 4-1. Individual Processing Systems

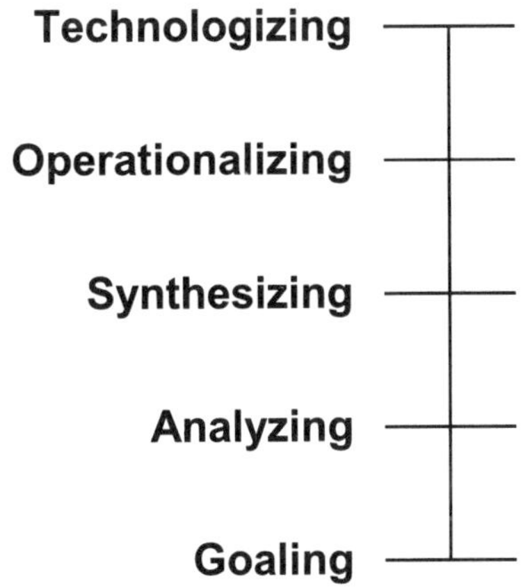

Goaling

Individual processing begins with **goaling.** The goaling systems emphasize our values (see Table 4-2). The values are the results outputs we wish to achieve and the resources we are willing to invest. In all instances, goaling emphasizes articulating and measuring values involving results outputs (RO) and resource inputs (RI). The values and their measures are as follows:

- **Performance**—Measures of individual performance at workstations based on comparing task inputs and outputs $\left(\frac{ro}{ri}\right)$;
- **Production**—Measures of unit production based on comparing unit inputs and outputs $\left(\frac{RO}{RI}\right)$;

- **Productivity**—Measures of systems' production based on comparing systems inputs and outputs (RO > RI);
- **Profit**—Measures of organizational performance based on comparing values of organizational inputs and outputs (\$RO > \$RI);
- **Profitability Growth**—Measures of organizational performance based on comparing the values of current performance and future potential $(\$RO > \$RI)^n > (\$RO > \$RI)^{n-1}$.

Table 4-2. Goaling by Measuring Values

VALUES	QUANTITATIVE MEASURES
• PROFIT GROWTH	$(\$RO > \$RI)^n > (\$RO > \$RI)^{n-1}$
• PROFIT	\$RO > \$RI
• PRODUCTIVITY	RO > RI
• PRODUCTION	$\frac{RO}{RI}$
• PERFORMANCE	$\frac{ro}{ri}$

In our own work, we have found that people get excited when they begin to understand the substance and system of goaling: *"If you don't know where you're going, you sure can't get there!"* It helps to know what the different levels of organizational goals are all about. Although people may change their goals over the course of processing, it helps to know what they intended to measure when they began.

Analyzing

Individual processing continues with **analyzing.** Analyzing emphasizes assessing the entity by *breaking it down* (dissecting it) into its systems dimensions: component inputs, procedural processes, function outputs, contextual conditions, and standards feedback (see Figure 4-7). The initial purpose of analyzing is to determine the level of goal achievement.

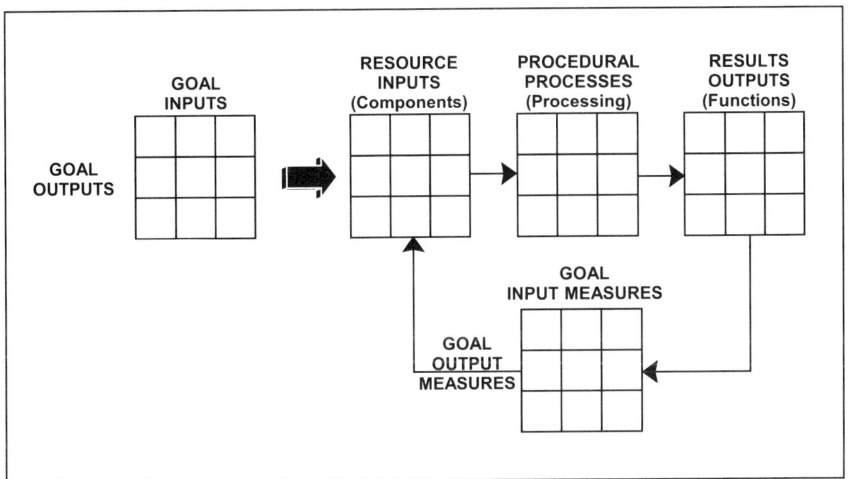

Figure 4-7. Analyzing by Dissembling Entities

Let us focus upon the analytic process. After establishing our goal measures for inputs and outputs, we may analyze our level of goal achievement against these standards $\left(\frac{\text{RO}}{\text{RI}}\right)$.

If our feedback is satisfactory, analysis is terminated. If it is unsatisfactory, our feedback initiates the next phase of analysis, in which we compare our outputs with our inputs to determine whether there were any deficits in either. If there were no deficits, we analyze the processes by which the inputs were transformed into the outputs. If any deficits in inputs, outputs, or processes are easily correctable and also acceptable, then we may terminate processing. If not, we will continue to the synthesizing phase.

In our own work, people have found that the threshold event of processing is analyzing. It is here that they face the *"Go—No Go"* decision: if they are satisfied with the level of goal achievement, it is *"No Go"*; if they are dissatisfied, it is *"Go!"* Our people like to label the products of analysis *"Current Operating Principles,"* or *"COPs."* In their experience, most *COPs* are *cop-outs:* if we are not willing to synthesize new operating principles, we are *copping out* on our goals.

Synthesizing

Individual processing continues with **synthesizing** to assemble new entities (see Figure 4-8). Synthesizing involves two operations: (1) expanding systems alternatives in order to discover new sources of dimensions; (2) narrowing the new dimensions in order to assemble new entities. Our new operations are calculated to impact our level of goal achievement.

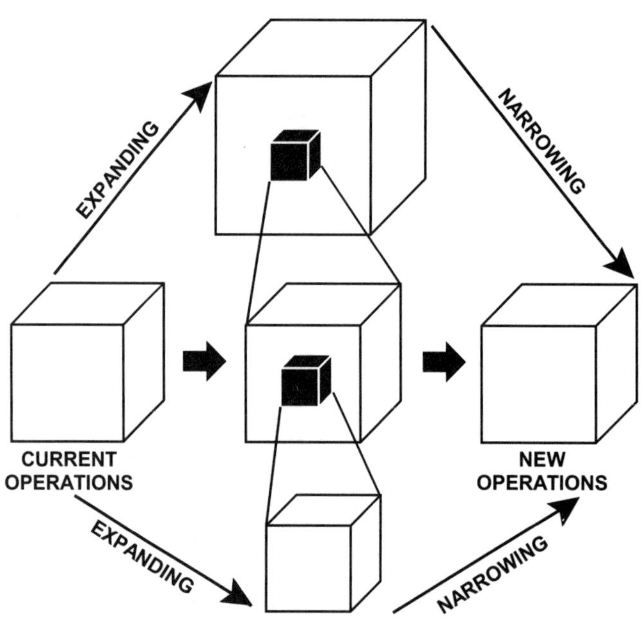

Figure 4-8. Synthesizing by Assembling New Entities

Synthesizing is the key to generativity. It is in the expanding and narrowing processes that we discover new and more powerful operations. For example, if we are analyzing a production system, we may explore alternative production systems and compare them to our current one. In further expanding, we may *"step up"* to include the intentions of our organizational architecture or alignment, and even *"step up"* to include the requirements of our organization's marketplace positioning. We may also expand by *"stepping down"* to generate new planning methods for achieving our objectives and/or new prototyping systems for implementing our programs. Finally, we will narrow to our preferred operations by employing our goaling measures.

Excitement builds as our people enter the synthesizing phase of processing. They are exhilarated by the possibilities generated by expanding. They are refocused by the probabilities generated by narrowing. Our people have found that one day of generative processing may accomplish more than a year of discriminative learning or a lifetime of conditioned responding. Our people like to label the products of this synthesis *"Possibilities Operating Principles,"* or *"POPs."* In their experience, all *POPs* are *pop-outs:* we *pop out* to more successful operations.

Operationalizing

Individual processing continues with **operationalizing:** developing rapid prototypes of new entities. Prototyping is defined in the same manner that we have defined all models and systems: by their operations (see Figure 4-9). The purpose of operationalizing is to define our images as achievable objectives.

We thus develop prototypes for achievable images by defining their operations: components, functions, processes, conditions, standards. Basically, we define *what* components will discharge *what* functions by *what* processes under *what* specifiable conditions and with *what* measurable standards.

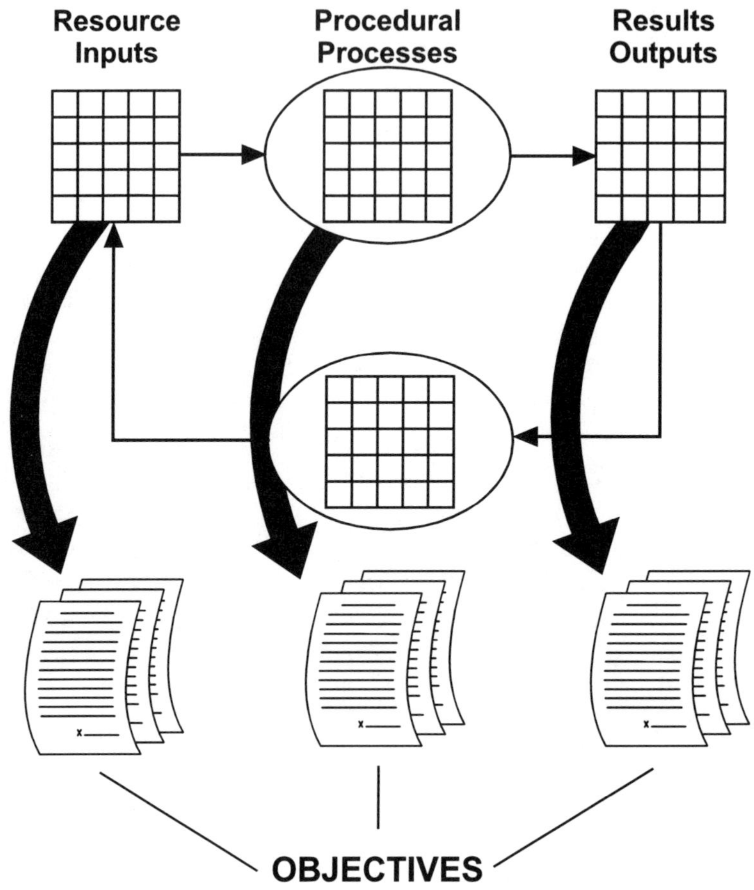

Figure 4-9. Operationalizing by Prototyping New Entities

Empowered by information relating and representing systems, operationalizing has become fluid and rapid for our personnel. Basically, by aligning functions, components, and processes, they develop rapid prototypes of entities. Our people like to label the products of operationalizing *"Probabilities Operations Principles,"* or *"POP IIs."* In their experience, *POP IIs* are guaranteed to be successful: *"Anything that can be defined can be achieved!"*

Technologizing

Finally, individual processing culminates with **technologizing** by programming new steps to accomplish new tasks. Programming is defined as systematic, step-by-step procedures that are implemented by specific task performance involving skills, knowledge, and attitudes (see Figure 4-10). The purpose of technologizing is to describe task performance in sufficient detail so objectives can be achieved.

Figure 4-10. Technologizing by Programmatically Developing New Products or Delivering New Services

Planning and implementing programs are, of course, areas of great expertise for all managers. There is one caveat: be aware of the continuously changing nature of all processes, including programs. With continuous processing, plans and programs may be continuously modified.

Finally, the product of our individual processing is a new phenomenal system (see Figure 4-11). After we have developed the programs to achieve the new objectives, we have new systems. These systems are elevated, or prime, images of the phenomena. For example, in human capital development, we may incorporate the following:

- New input objectives for evaluating the recruitment of technically skilled human resources;
- New process objectives for empowering people in generative processing systems;

- New output objectives for retaining human capital.

In other words, we may transform our current HRD models into HCD models.

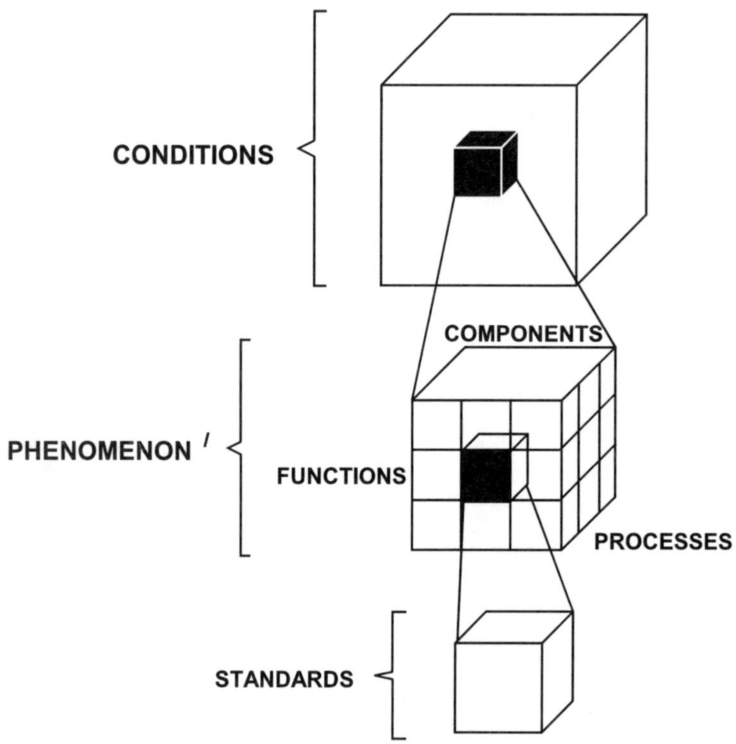

Figure 4-11. New Phenomenon

In the final analysis, we transform our current images of phenomena to prime images. Indeed, we continuously transform our current images into more powerful images. To be sure, our people are fond of saying, *"There is no plan—only processing!"* However, there is indeed a plan—a plan for continuous interdependent processing!

The Generative Thinker

Jesse embarked on his search for *"best processes"* to generate innovations. Here is what he discovered.

First, the discriminative-learning practices of his engineering group were not that bad. They could be summarized as:

1. Formulating goals,
2. Analyzing current operations,
3. Adopting *"current practices."*

However, Jesse knew that these learning practices certainly were not good enough to meet the spiraling requirements of the marketplace.

Second, the phases of generative processing were defined as follows:

1. **Goaling** values,
2. **Analyzing** current operations,
3. **Synthesizing** productive operations,
4. **Operationalizing** productive operations,
5. **Technologizing** productive operations.

Known by the acronym *"GASOT,"* the generative processing system exchanged *"best practices"* for *"best processes."*

Jesse learned that the source of generative processing was the *nesting* of all discriminative learning systems within the human processor's system:

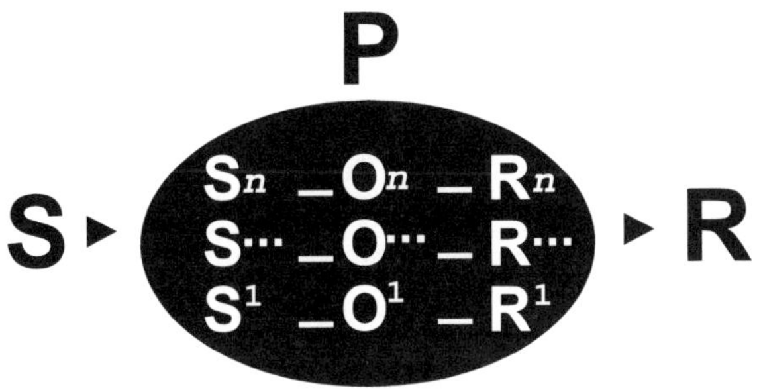

P

S ▸ $S^n - O^n - R^n$ / $S^{\cdots} - O^{\cdots} - R^{\cdots}$ / $S^1 - O^1 - R^1$ ▸ R

We may translate the above image in this way: basically, the human processor is the repository of a hierarchy of discriminative learning systems (S-O-R); upon presentation of the stimulus (S), the processor (P) relates permutations and combinations of S-O-R systems to generate entirely new responses (R).

Jesse could see that the synthesizing phase of processing was the key to generating new images of outputs. It is during this phase that we first expand and then narrow alternative operations. We expand in terms of our knowledgeability of *"best practices"* or *"best ideas."* As shown in the following illustration, we view management-systems problems from above by expanding to executive architecture and policymaking. Maybe changes made at the top can resolve the problems at the systems level. We also view systems from below by expanding to supervisor and delivery levels. Maybe changes made at the bottom can resolve systems problems.

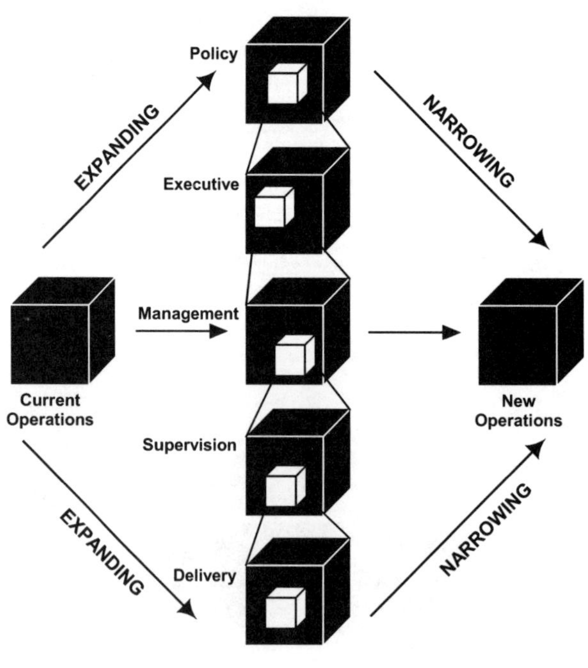

Jesse understood that this is precisely where information modeling comes in. The productivity of our expanding is a function of the utility of our modeling. Whether we adopt legacy models or develop entirely new models will determine our ability to generate or innovate in processing. Here we must rely upon our information-modeling skills to develop interdependent, multidimensional, and ever changing models for consideration. In the final analysis, it is the permutations and combinations of these models that generate the most productive operating systems.

Jesse also understood that the expanding operations are followed by narrowing operations. These narrowing operations reflect the values that went into the development of our goals. They may also reflect the continuous growth of our values and our continuously changing goals. Goals and operations are *"moving targets"*—changeable goals and changeable operations.

In applying what he had discovered about processing and operations, Jesse came to learn even more. For example, let us see what happened when Jesse addressed his current images of the engineering group.

Basically, the group was a centralized and integrated operation. As shown in the next illustration, its functions emphasized the systems level down; its components were sales-engineering-driven technology and production units; its processes emphasized inputting, planning, and outputting. Jesse summarized the current operations of the engineering group in this way:

> *Systems designs are generated by sales-driven technology and production units empowered by processing, planning, and outputting.*

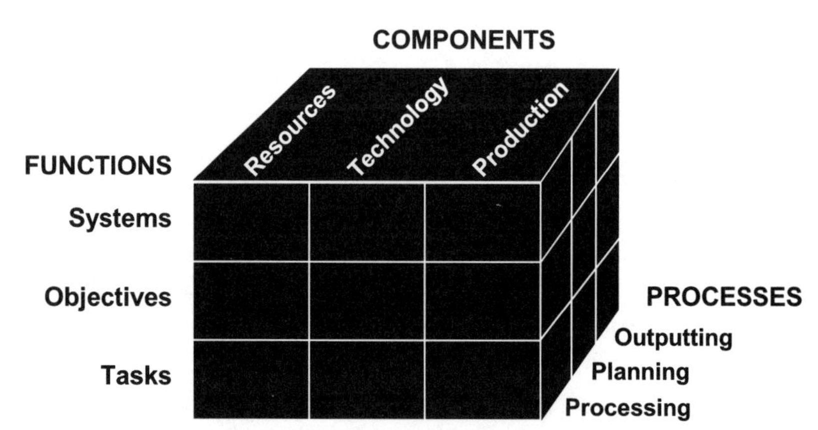

Jesse decided that the engineering group was primarily a planning unit. He had a good image of how to plan:

- Define the goals;
- Design the systems;
- Derive the objectives;
- Detail the tasks.

Defensively he would say, *"This works for me!"* But in his open moments, he realized that time-to-market was the critical variable: his people no longer had "turnaround time" from customer requirements to engineering products. He soon confessed, *"It no longer works so well!"*

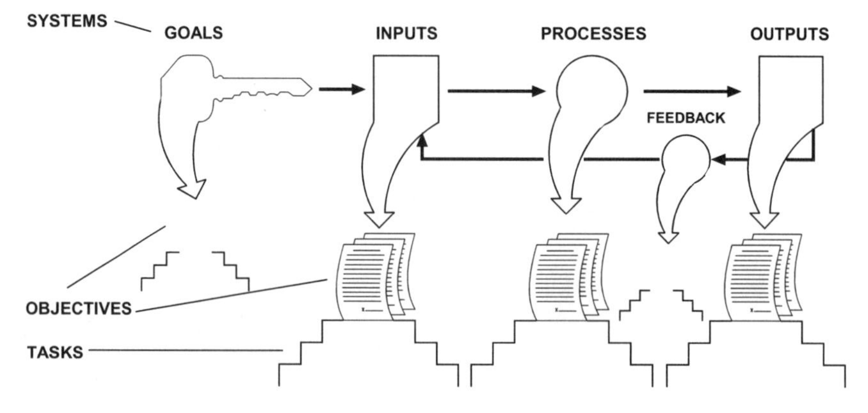

To programmatically expand alternative operations, Jesse incorporated transfer matrices. At the systems level, he held one or more of the operations constant while varying the other operations:

- Goaling,
- Inputting,
- Processing,
- Planning,
- Outputting.

That way he could programmatically search out new sources of improved operations.

SYSTEMS

OPERATIONS	**Goals**	**Inputs**	**Processes**	**Plans**	**Outputs**
Goals					
Inputs					
Processes					
Plans					
Outputs					

Jesse also installed transfer matrices at the objectives level, systematically holding constant and varying dimensions in order to search out more productive dimensions:

- Functions,
- Components,
- Processes,
- Conditions,
- Standards.

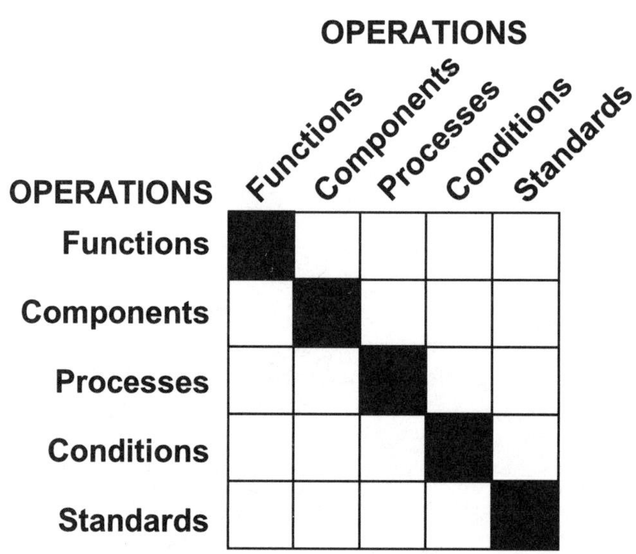

Here is what this powerful processing yielded for Jesse and his engineering group:

1. He redefined sales engineering as resource integration and made it the driving unit: the people of this unit were placed as close as possible to the users of the equipment to enable them to more accurately tailor designs to customer requirements.
2. He introduced generative processing as the driver of the processing system: processing meant receiving and processing the inputs to generate the most powerful images of the designs.
3. He decentralized the operations and rotated the levels of the functional systems, making different units responsible for different levels of functions:
   - Systems design was directed by the resource-integration unit enabled by generative processing.
   - Objective achievement was directed by the technology unit enabled by customized planning systems.

- Task performance was directed by the production unit enabled by standardized outputting systems.

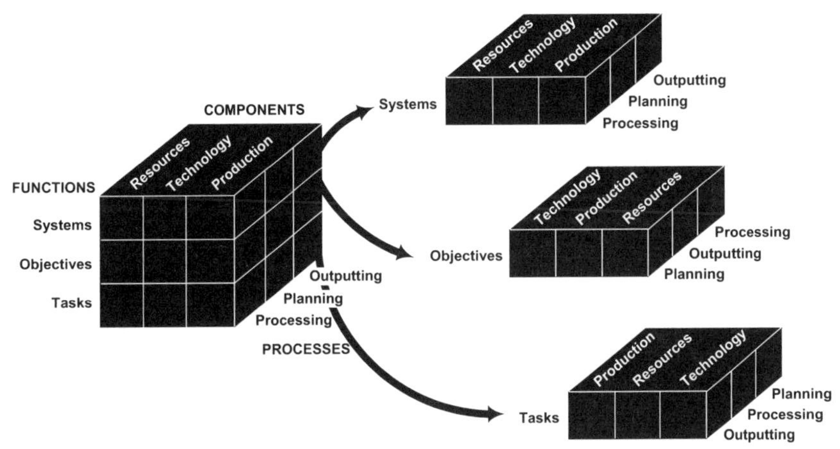

Jesse resolved that all of the people in all of the units would be empowered in S-P-R generative processing systems. That way, anyone and everyone could contribute to productivity improvement.

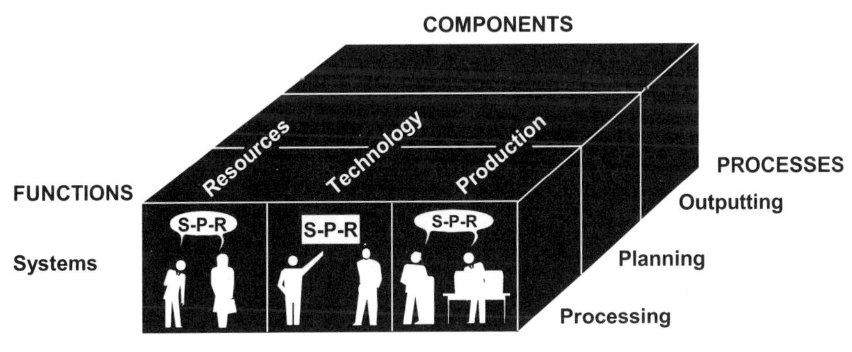

IN TRANSITION

Almost everything we do requires generative processing. Before we get together for processing in a group or unit, we should process individually. Indeed, we should *ante up* for interpersonal processing by generating our own images in individual processing.

A valuable tool for managing I^3 is presented in Table 4-3. With this tool, we can assess our employees' levels of processing different phenomena:

1. Have our employees established goals for the phenomena?
2. Have they analyzed the phenomena, breaking them down into their critical operations?
3. Have they synthesized new phenomena, putting new operations together in new ways?
4. Have they operationally defined the new phenomena?
5. Have they technologized the programs to achieve the new phenomena?

Table 4-3. I^3 Management Systems

LEVELS OF I^3	AREAS OF PHENOMENA		
	People	Data	Things
5. Technologizing			
4. Operationalizing			
3. Synthesizing			
2. Analyzing			
1. Goaling			

The answers to these questions will dictate our level of confidence in our employees and in the phenomena they have processed at this level.

Case: The Possibilities Leader (continued)

Through her experience in the individual processing phase, Sharon Fisher came to realize two essential points:

- *Our ability to process generatively is contingent upon our ability to model dimensionally.* Only with skills in information representing can we expand our operations alternatives; only with skills in information representing can we narrow the alternatives to the most highly leveraged operations. As Fisher concluded, *generativity in thinking is a function of dimensionality in modeling.*
- *Processing is prepotent among all skills:* it is all-powerful in generating new ways of doing new things.

  For example, during this phase, Fisher never felt "boxed-in" by the problems confronting her. Now she was confident that she could enter *any* situation and generate "a better idea"—for she had "a better process."

Indeed, processing is simply more potent than the problems we face. To be sure, processing is what makes people feel potent!

In short, dimensionalized information is transformed into still more robust and productive information by generative individual processing systems: goaling, analyzing, synthesizing, operationalizing, technologizing—or GASOT (see Figure 4-12). In addition, the ongoing systems of information relating and information representing contribute developmentally and cumulatively to elevated communication for processing purposes. In other words, empathic relating and accurate information modeling continue to elevate our understanding of the complexity and power of the phenomena. In this way, individual processing prepares us for interpersonal processing: the skills to process interpersonally in an organizational context.

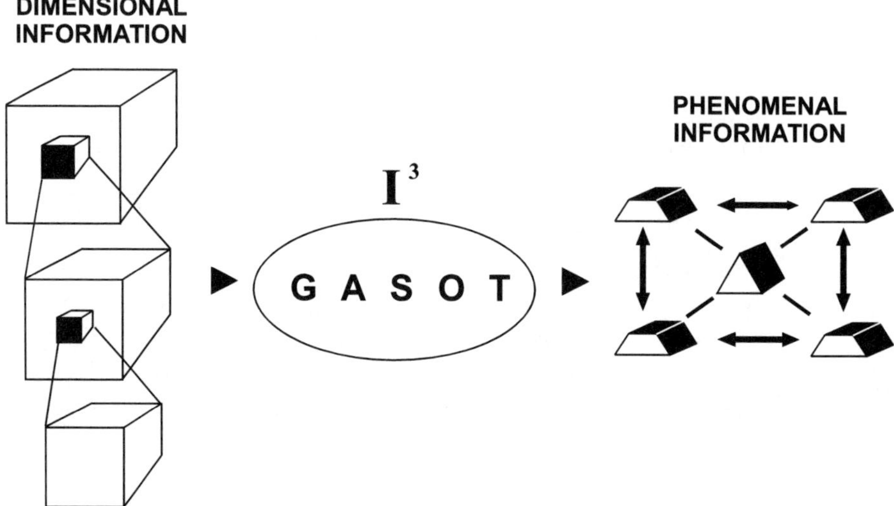

Figure 4-12. Individual Processing Systems

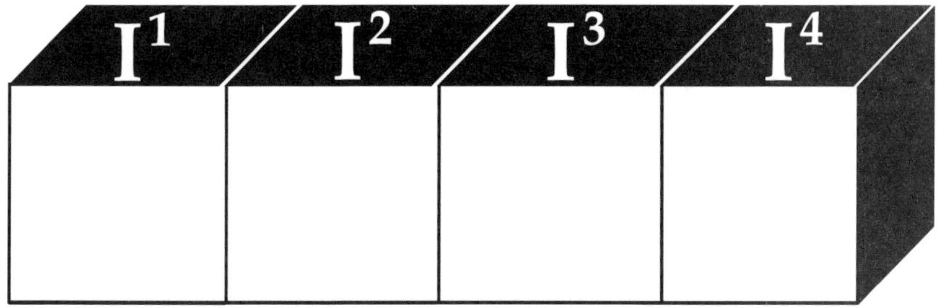

5 I⁴—Interpersonal Processing Systems

Interpersonal processing is the source of phenomenal processing for mutual benefit.

Individual processing empowers us to process generatively in groups. Put another way, before we can process interpersonally, we must process individually. We *"ante up"* to participate in interpersonal processing by generating our own individual images of our phenomena. We share these images with each other before proceeding to process new images together. We do all of our interpersonal processing systematically. Otherwise, we are in danger of *"brainstorming"*: literally storming or assaulting our brainpower by contributing random images to a random process.

Case: The Possibilities Leader
— I^4 *Interpersonal Processing*

Equipped with the phenomenal images generated by individual processing, Sharon Fisher was prepared for interpersonal processing. She related with co-workers "up, down, and sideways," employing her interpersonal processing systems:

- **Goaling** by measuring values,
- **Getting** others' images of the organization,
- **Giving** one's own image of the organization,
- **Growing** new images of the organization,
- **Going** on to implement the new images.

As a result, the group of co-workers expanded the initial corporate mission (see Figure 5-1), altering it to incorporate the following:

- Private-sector targets,
- Software-product and -services goals,
- Organizational strategies driven by research and development (R and D).

Together, Fisher and the others summarized the newly redefined mission:

> *Consulting, training, and software goals are accomplished with private- and public-sector targets by way of R-and-D-driven strategies.*

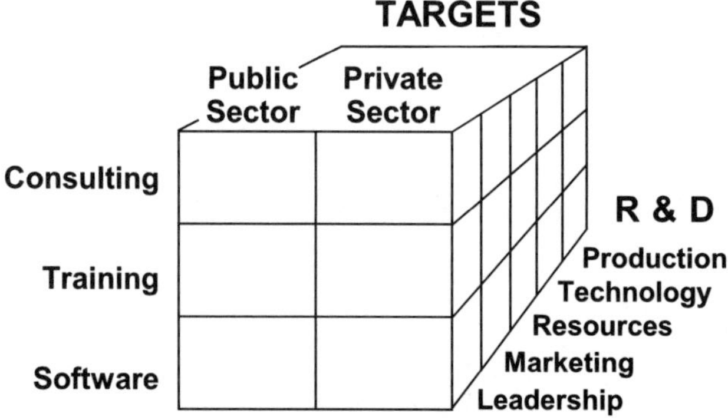

Figure 5-1. The Expanded Mission

Fisher continued to employ her interpersonal processing systems **to get** the others' images of the organization (see Figure 5-2). Here it is important to understand that the

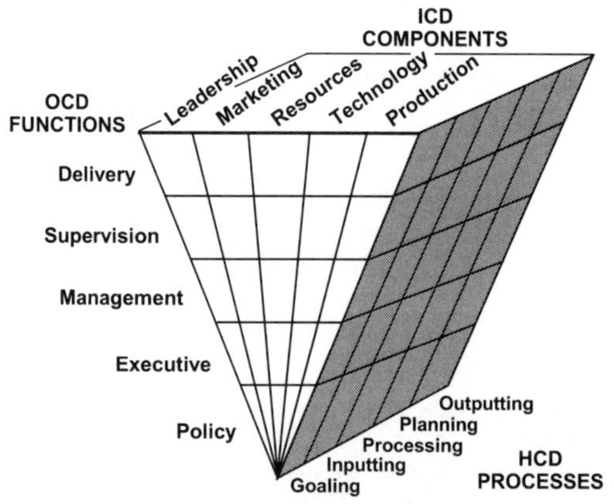

Figure 5-2. Getting Organizational Images

co-workers had engaged in individual processing on their own before entering interpersonal processing. One of their major insights was to invert the organization. This placed the delivery people at the source of ongoing information bulletins. They believed this was most appropriate in a service industry.

Next, Fisher used her interpersonal processing skills **to give** her own image of organizational operations (see Figure 5-3). Here she shared with the group the image that she had generated in individual processing—an organizational image centralized by mission and decentralized by operations.

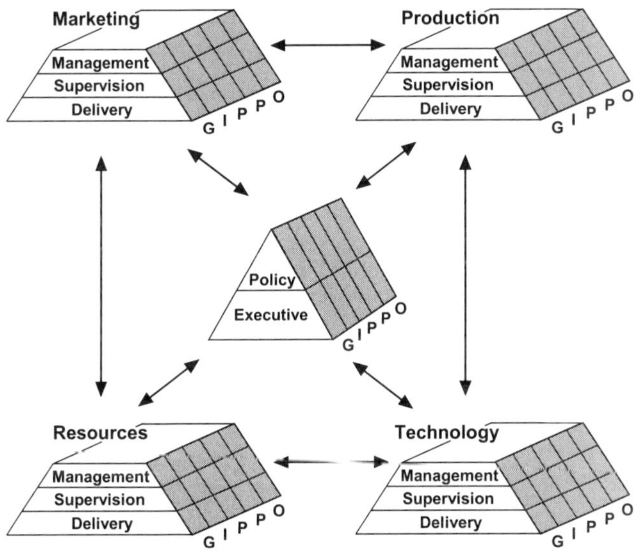

Figure 5-3. Giving Organizational Images

She and the group then employed their interpersonal processing skills **to grow** a new image of organizational operations (see Figure 5-4). This was the major work of interpersonal processing: using various images as input to generate entirely new images of organizational operations. We can describe those operations as:

- Centralized by mission,
- Decentralized by operations,
- Complemented by partnerships,
- Inverted where appropriate,
- Teamed where appropriate.

Together, our interpersonal processors had generated a *possibilities organization:* an organization that could instantaneously configure its functions, components, and processes to meet any changing market conditions and human standards.

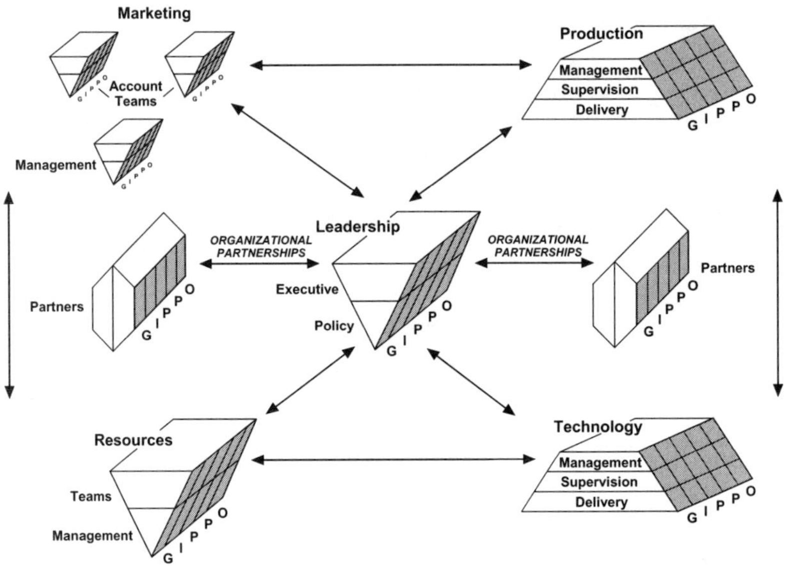

Figure 5-4. Growing New Organizational Images

Finally, the group employed interpersonal processing skills **to go** on to plan implementation of the new organizational model (see Figure 5-5). Members processed, among many technological nuances, entities such as inverted teaming. Here teams are in the lead positions to receive information, to process it, and to initiate. In turn, management is cast in a support role for higher-order processing.

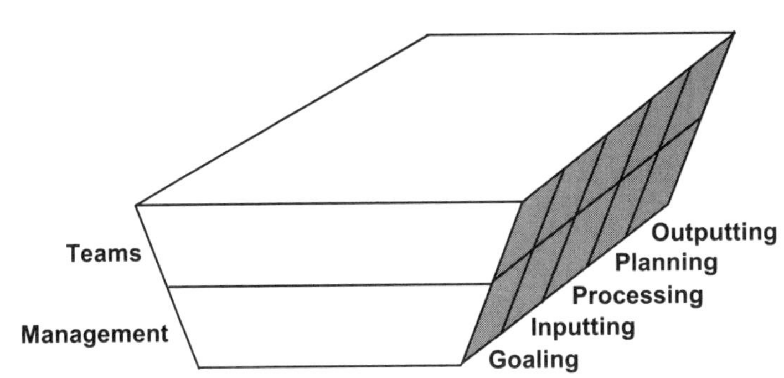

Figure 5-5. Going on to Technologize New Images

At this point in processing, Fisher's group was ready to implement an improved organizational model that included:

- I^1 *Operational phenomena,*
- I^2 *Dimensional phenomena,*
- I^3 *Generative phenomena,*
- I^4 *Improved generative phenomena.*

Moreover, they were committed to continuous interdependent processing to improve the model to meet the changing requirements of the marketplace.

INTERPERSONAL PROCESSING SYSTEMS

Possibilities management is, fourthly, a social science. With the brainpower of possibilities managers skilled in interpersonal processing, the phenomena can grow. In this manner, both manager and phenomena elevate a *process-to-process* dialogue to reach a *critical mass* of processing. It is this critical mass that reveals the principles of growth for both manager and phenomena.

The goal of interpersonal processing systems is to generate the most powerful, or prime, images of the phenomena; in other words, we transform our phenomenal images into prime phenomenal images (see Figure 5-6). Note that the phenomenal images are represented by the decentralized organizational images. In turn, the prime phenomenal images are represented by a mix of decentralized relationships: the nature of the operations depends upon their functions. This is a ***"possibilities organization."*** It is generated by interpersonal processing systems. It is continuously upgraded by continuous interdependent processing, or I^5.

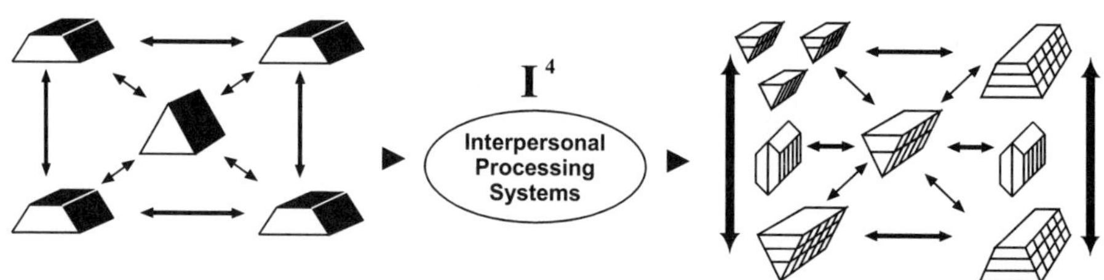

Figure 5-6. Interpersonal Processing Systems

Let us put interpersonal processing into the perspective of the social sciences. So-called experts have espoused many different kinds of interpersonal-relating approaches in management. Basically, these approaches are either (1) authoritarian, or manager-centered; (2) employee-, or customer-, centered; or (3) situation-centered. The truth is this: ***none of these relate!***

The authoritarian approach assumes the critical expertise of the manager. With the spiraling changes that are taking place, this is rare. Indeed, as a general rule, expertise is a function of dedication and concentration. And more often than not, the expertise is found in someone else's brainpower. We call this authoritarian approach *"Give and Go!"* The managers *give* the orders, and the employees *go*—attempt to perform them. Even when the manager has expertise, this approach is problematic because the parties involved never get an opportunity to agree upon the tasks.

The employee-centered approach, on the other hand, assumes that critical expertise is in the other person. We call this approach *"Get and Go!"* The managers *get* the direction from employees, who *go* on to perform the tasks. Even when other people have expertise, they do not benefit from the manager's perspectives in relaying the unit's requirements for performing the tasks.

The Situational Manager

It is legendary in manufacturing that the drivers of products are quality, cost, and timeliness. *"Pick two"* is the adage. Tom wanted all three: increasingly high-quality, innovative products and decreasing costs and time-to-market. To pursue this end, he met with his group leaders in production.

Basically, at that point Tom had three management models to choose from. The first model was authoritarian: Tom could *give* directions to his group. We call this the *"Give and Go"* approach: the manager *gives* the orders and the people *go out* and follow them. This model assumes that the expertise resides in the manager—a flawed assumption at best! The manager is regarded, explicitly or implicitly, as the exemplary performer.

The second model reflected Tom's intuitively democratic values: he could *get* directions from his group. We label this the *"Get and Go"* approach: the manager *gets* the directions from the group, and the group *goes out* and follows them. This model assumes that the expertise resides in the group members—something that may be a shaky assumption. The manager is reduced to relating, more or less!

The third model was a sharing and consensus-building model: Tom and his group could share images of responses and negotiate a merged image of a consensus response. We term this the *"Get, Give, Merge, and Go"* approach: the manager *gets* and then *gives* images before leading the group to a *merged* image. This model assumes that the expertise resides somewhere between the manager and the group members. The manager is reduced to a facilitator, more or less!

Tom was able to detect the problem inherent in the third model: the decision-making involved in merging images was just another version of consensus-building—group members would generate images individually, only to see them disappear or converge in consensus-building. That made no sense to Tom.

"The very reason why we introduced individual processing was to avoid consensus-building," he reminded his group leaders. *"So why would we now submit these individual images to a consensus-building process? Moreover, there is* ***no processing.****"*

Tom realized that we can process interpersonally only when we assume expertise is *"somewhere"* in a group. We thus process interpersonally in the same manner that we processed individually: by goaling, analyzing, synthesizing, operationalizing, and technologizing. Tom resolved to learn how to process interpersonally.

He soon found out there was also a *processing* approach: he and group members could process together after sharing images derived from individual processing. We term this approach *"Get, Give, Grow, and Go."* The manager *gets* and *gives* images before leading the group in *growing:* processing to generate entirely new images. This model assumes the expertise lies out there somewhere and that group members will engage in a process to find it. The manager is elevated to processor—interpersonal processor.

Tom concluded: *"Let's face it, no one knows everything—things are changing too rapidly. But we can all do one thing—process!"*

Interpersonal Processing Skills

In interpersonal processing, processing grows to a critical mass: it interactively bridges *neuronal gaps* in all participants by generating insights that were previously unavailable. The possibilities manager is now empowered to invest more enlightened resources in future *developmental mergers*.

Interpersonal processing systems are scaled as shown in Table 5-1. We describe these systems as follows:

- **Goaling** by measuring values,
- **Getting** by responding to others' images of entities,
- **Giving** by initiating our images of entities,
- **Growing** by generating new images of entities,
- **Going** by acting to develop new entities.

Table 5-1. Interpersonal Processing Systems

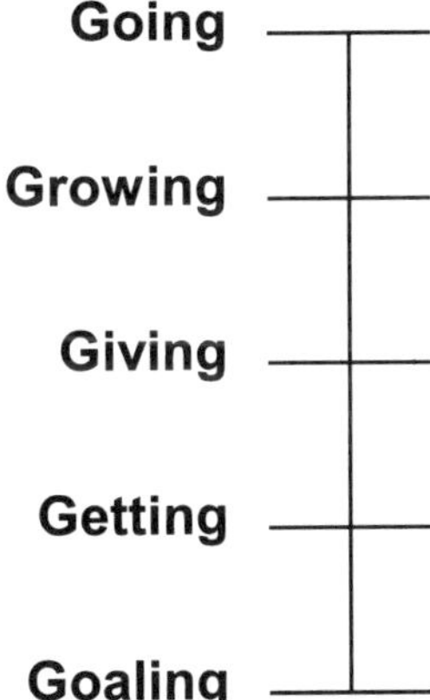

Goaling

The goaling operations are the same as those of individual generative processing systems. The only difference is that now the goals of multiple parties—possibly representing different areas of expertise or assignment—are articulated and measured. Table 5-2 exhibits some qualitative measures of goals. As shown, there is a correspondence of measures to organizational level.

Table 5-2. Goaling by Organizational Levels

Level	Goal	Measure
POLICY	Profit growth,	or $(\$RO > \$RI)^n > (\$RO > \$RI)^{n-1}$
EXECUTIVE	Profit,	or $\$RO > \$RI$
MANAGEMENT	Productivity,	or $RO > RI$
SUPERVISION	Production,	or $\frac{RO}{RI}$
DELIVERY	Performance,	or $\frac{ro}{ri}$

Getting

Here the managers respond to *get* the processors' images of the entities (see Figure 5-7). Attempts are made to *get* all of the images of all of the parties involved.

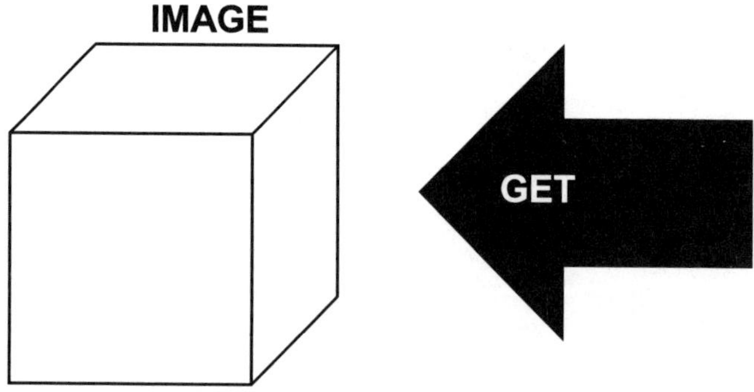

Figure 5-7. Getting by Responding to Images of Entities

When *getting,* we can use the skills that we learned in information relating: attending, responding, personalizing, and initiating. These relating skills enable us to facilitate *getting* the images of others.

Giving

The managers now *give* their images of the entities, presenting the images from their own frames of reference (see Figure 5-8). By including the images of others, the processors should be able to *give* prime, or improved, images of the entities.

Figure 5-8. Giving by Initiating Images of Entities

When *giving,* we can use the dimensionalizing skills that we learned in information representing: 1D, 2D, 3D, *Nested*-D, and Multi-D. These representing skills enable us to facilitate *giving* our images of the phenomena.

Growing

Both managers and employees now *grow,* or *generate,* to develop new images by processing together (see Figure 5-9). In this way, they produce a new, *shared* image of the entities.

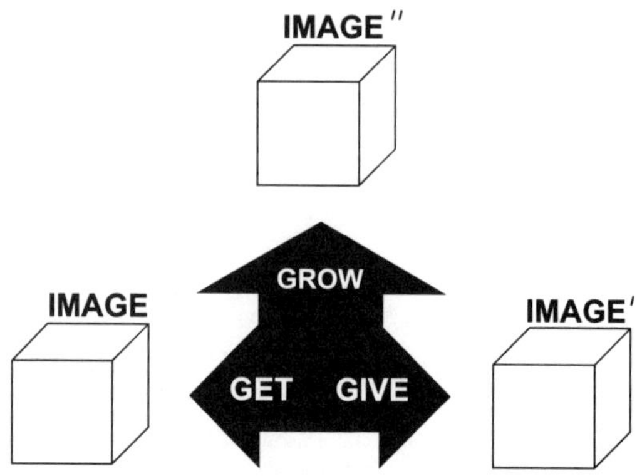

Figure 5-9. Growing by Generating New Images of Entities

When *growing,* we can use the skills that we learned in individual processing: goaling, analyzing, synthesizing, operationalizing, and technologizing. These processing skills enable us to *generate* new images of the phenomena.

Going

Finally, managers and their employees *go* on, acting to achieve the new images of the entities (see Figure 5-10).

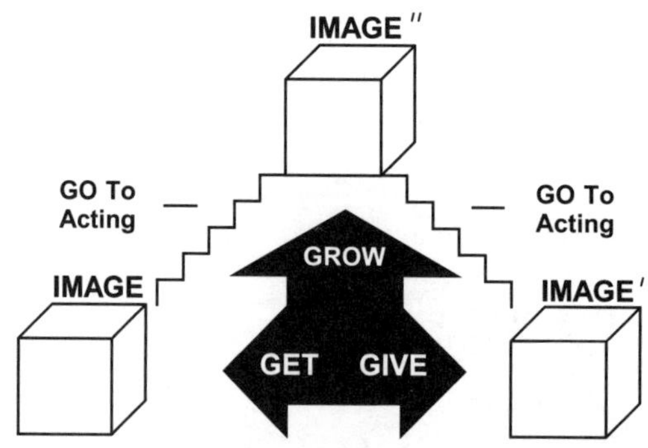

Figure 5-10. Going on by Planning to Achieve New Entities

Here we can use the manager's special areas of expertise, planning and producing: operationally defining objectives, systematically programming steps to achieve the objectives, and diligently performing the tasks to implement the programs. These planning skills enable us to facilitate *going* on to implement our new images of the phenomena.

The key to interpersonal processing is found in individual processing. All participants *ante up* with the images they have generated individually; then they participate in interpersonal processing. At this stage, to process interpersonally, they may matrix individual and interpersonal processing operations as illustrated in Table 5-3.

Table 5-3. Interpersonal Processing Systems

Individual Processing Systems \ Interpersonal Processing Systems	Goaling	Getting	Giving	Growing	Going
Technologizing					
Operationalizing					
Synthesizing					
Analyzing					
Goaling					

In practice, we align our interpersonal processing systems with the function of discharging the operations of our individual processing systems; this is illustrated next, in Table 5-4. As may be noted, we *"Goal, Get, Give, Grow, and Go"* (GGGGG) for every phase of I^3.

Table 5-4. I^4 x I^3

INTERPERSONAL PROCESSING SYSTEMS		INDIVIDUAL PROCESSING SYSTEMS
GGGGG	—	Goaling
GGGGG	—	Analyzing
GGGGG	—	Synthesizing
GGGGG	—	Operationalizing
GGGGG	—	Technologizing

As may also be noted, we move through the phases of individual processing in order, from Goaling through Technologizing, addressing one phase before proceeding to the next.

The Interpersonal Manager

Tom and his group discovered that interpersonal processing was a way of life. They learned there were three functions of this form of processing: *"best practices," "best ideas,"* and *"best processes."*

Over time, Tom utilized all three functions, separately or in combination. He made these distinctions between them:

- ***"Best practices"*** was a consensus-building process: the team got together to share images of the products or practices. Tom employed the interpersonal processing systems accordingly: *getting* and *giving* images before negotiating *merged* images of the *"best practice."*

  He found this *"Get, Give, Merge"* consensus-building approach most appropriate when *timeliness* was important.

- ***"Best ideas"*** was an ideational process: the team got together to share images and then generate new images of the products or practices. Tom employed the interpersonal processing systems accordingly: *getting* and *giving* images before *growing* new images of the best practices.

  He found this *"Get, Give, Grow"* ideational approach most appropriate when *quality* was most important.

- ***"Best processes"*** was an ongoing, generative process: the team got together on a periodic basis—members processed interpersonally, dispersed to process individually, and then got together again. Tom employed the interpersonal processing systems accordingly: *getting* and *giving* before *growing; growing* before *getting* and *giving.*

  He found this *"Get, Give, Grow and Grow and Grow"* generative approach most appropriate when they were *"betting the business on it."*

Overall, Tom favored the *"best processes"* approach. It not only generated the *best ideas,* but also negotiated the *best practices* along the way. Most important, the *"Grow and Grow"* approach was proactive. It enabled his team to stay on the "cutting edge"—to keep their business *in business!*

IN TRANSITION

The threshold phase of interpersonal processing is found in *growing,* in processing generatively together. We anté up with individual processing. However, we generate the power of our play with interpersonal growing.

A system for managing I^4 is shown in Table 5-5. As illustrated, the interpersonal processing systems are dedicated to the generative processing operations: goaling, analyzing, synthesizing, operationalizing, technologizing. Again, we may assess our employees' levels of processing different phenomena:

1. Have our employees processed growth goals interpersonally?
2. Have they analyzed the phenomena interpersonally?
3. Have they synthesized new phenomena interpersonally?
4. Have they operationally defined the new phenomena interpersonally?
5. Have they technologized the programs interpersonally?

Table 5-5. I^4 Management Systems

LEVELS OF I^4	AREAS OF PHENOMENA		
	People	**Data**	**Things**
5. GGGGG - Technologizing			
4. GGGGG - Operationalizing			
3. GGGGG - Synthesizing			
2. GGGGG - Analyzing			
1. GGGGG - Goaling			

The answers to these questions will dictate our confidence in our people as well as in the phenomena they generate.

Case: The Possibilities Leader (continued)

The I^4 phase led to many discoveries for Sharon Fisher and her group. One of the most exciting was that interpersonal processing applications can take a multitude of forms, depending on the diversity of the interpersonal processors and their skills. For instance, further generative interpersonal processing generated images of possibilities organizations such as the one presented in Figure 5-11. A possibilities organization is capable of instantaneously aligning resources to serve continuously changing policy.

In the illustration, the policymaking function and the leadership component are decentralized to provide maximum horizontal and vertical integration in leadership. Similarly, the technology and production components are decentralized to maximize the integration of information modeling and mechanical tooling. Finally, the marketing components and delivery functions are decentralized to address special needs.

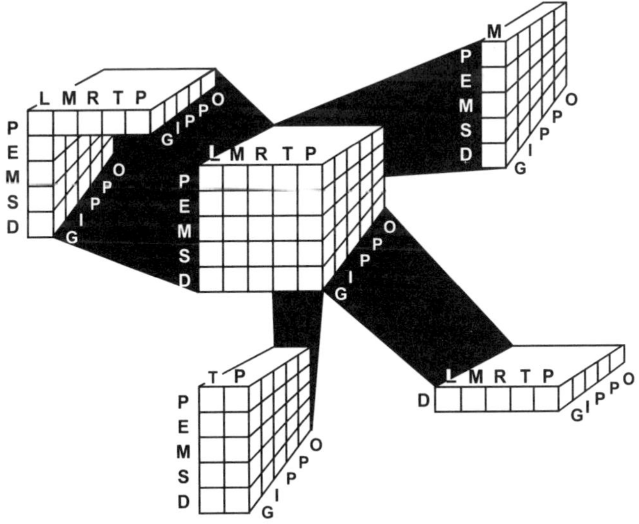

Figure 5-11. An Illustration of a Possibilities Organization

Discovering the diversity of productive images that interpersonal processing generates is an exhilarating experience for our people. The *possibilizing* of all phenomena is only one illustration. In interaction with individual processing, interpersonal processing empowers our people to grow, and grow, and grow. Each new experience with each new phenomenon—people, data, things—is an opportunity to grow.

The purpose of interpersonal processing is to leverage the potentially multiplicative effects of individual processing. In short, our people find that interpersonal processing, used facilitatively, compounds the effect of individual processing. What one can do, more can do much better! This is because empowered people have *"a better process."*

In short, interpersonal processing systems may transform multidimensional information into *possibilities information* (Figure 5-12). Indeed, interpersonal processing prepares us for phenomenal processing: the skills to process in all phenomenal contexts.

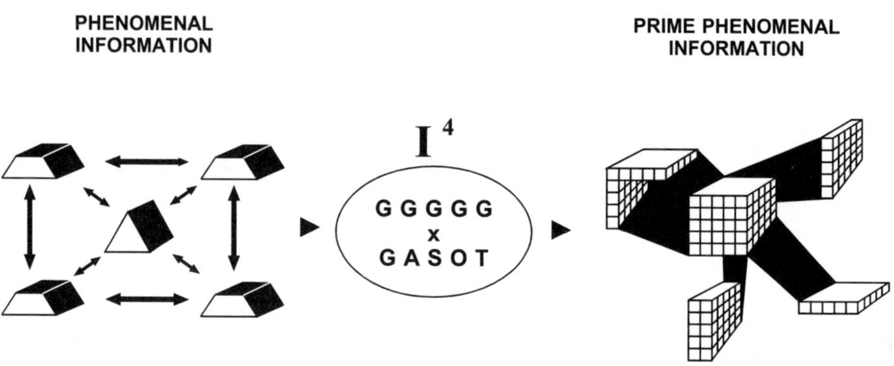

Figure 5-12. Interpersonal Processing Systems

Just as others intervene to accomplish complex tasks, so we intervene to actualize probabilities science by interpersonal processing. Imagine, actualizing the possibilities of probabilities!

6 I^5—Interdependent Processing Systems

Interdependent processing is the continuing source of generativity.

Interpersonal processing empowers us to process interdependently. Interdependent processing means becoming *"one"* with the phenomena we are addressing. In the case of organizational phenomena, it means becoming one with the organization's sources of new capital development:

- Marketplace capital development, or marketplace positioning;
- Organizational capital development, or alignment of the organization with marketplace positioning;
- Human capital development, or generative human processing to align with the organization;
- Information capital development, or generative human processing to align with the organization;
- Information capital development, or information modeling to enable human processing;
- Mechanical capital development, or mechanical tooling to implement information modeling.

Interdependent processing with organizational phenomena is the source of all new capital development.

Case: The Possibilities Leader

— I^5 *Interdependent Processing*

Now empowered by the image of *"the possibilities organization,"* Sharon Fisher and her colleagues were able to *nest* the organization inside marketplace conditions, as shown in Figure 6-1. Note that the possibilities organization was designed to be aligned with marketplace positioning. Fisher and her group then prepared to *nest* inside the possibilities organization all those requirements for generating organizational capital: human processing, information modeling, mechanical tooling.

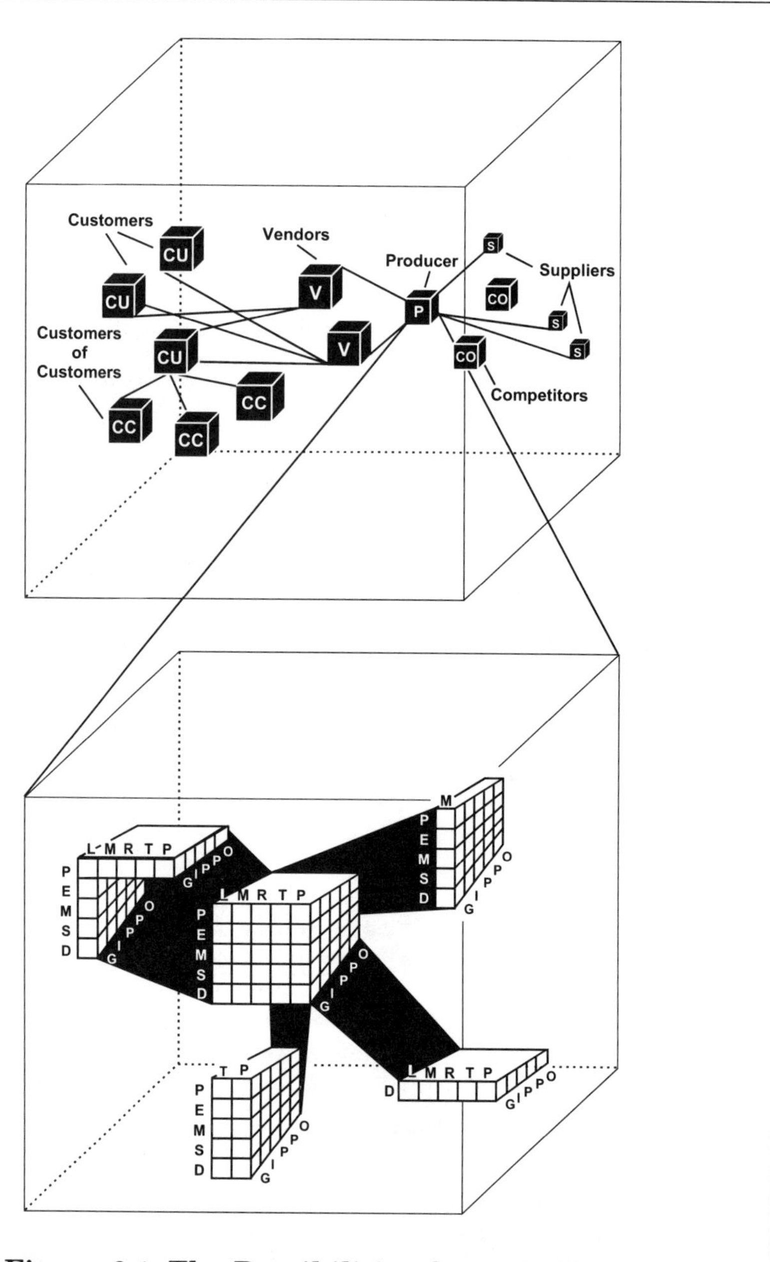

Figure 6-1. The Possibilities Organization *Nested* Within Marketplace Positioning

This meant that each level of new capital development was contingent upon every other level. Clearly, marketplace positioning required organizational alignment to become marketplace capital. That was the mission of Fisher and company's interdependent-processing effort. Similarly, "the possibilities organization" could be converted to organizational capital only with successful human processing. Likewise, human processing could become human capital only with effective information modeling. Finally, information modeling could become information capital only with productive mechanical tooling.

Fisher and her group realized that these forms of new capital development are not static, but continuously changing, and so managers are continuously processing. They also realized the implications of this for the managers in their organization: now that those managers had helped to generate "the possibilities organization" design, they had to learn to live and work within that design in order to generate organizational capital. Above all, they had to engage in continuous interdependent processing—with one another and with the phenomena.

With this in mind, the group worked on the concept of processing teams, representing them by the interpersonal processing model shown in Figure 6-2. We can see that the individual

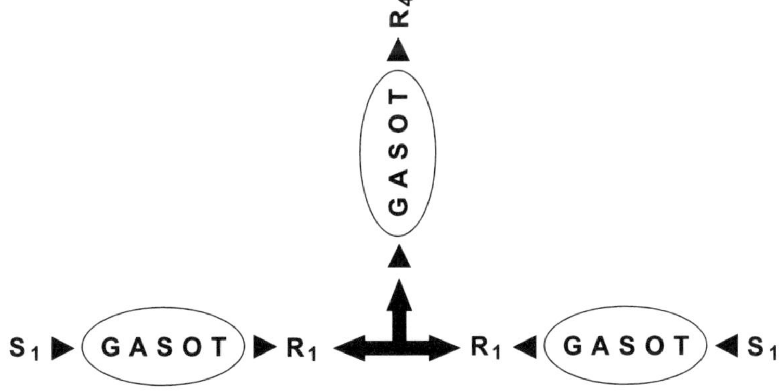

Figure 6-2. Processing Teams

processors process independently before coming together to process interpersonally. Note that the teams can generate at least four generations of responses (R^4) in a relatively brief period of time.

Next, these interpersonal processing teams were *nested* within the phenomenal systems (see Figure 6-3). The mission was continuous interdependent processing with the phenomenal systems; thus, the interpersonal processing teams would bring their leveraged potential to bear upon the interdependent processing mission. In this manner, the group generated a design for organization capital development.

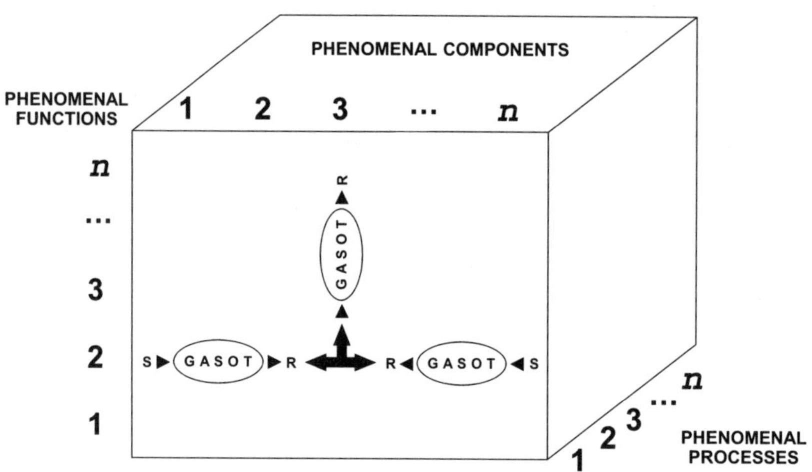

Figure 6-3. Interdependent Processing Teams *Nested* Within Phenomenal Systems

Fisher and company now addressed the issue of human capital. They realized that human processing required information modeling to become such capital. Accordingly, Fisher introduced NCD-systems modeling to increase the potential alternative images of the interdependent processing teams. We can see this modeling in Figure 6-4.

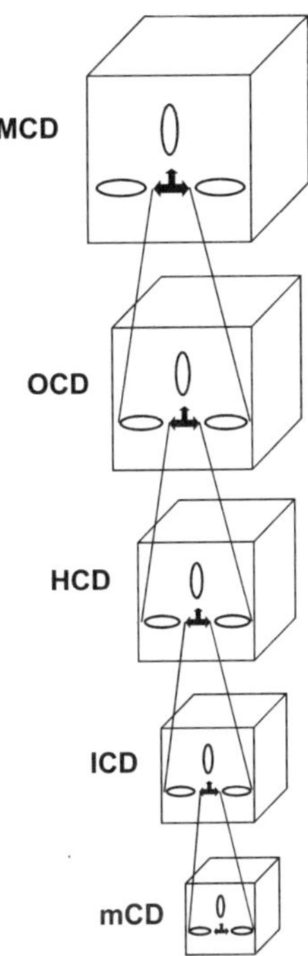

Figure 6-4. Interpersonal Processing Within New Capital Development Systems

Notice that the higher-order levels of new capital development *nest* the lower-order levels of MCD to mCD:

- MCD—Marketplace capital development, or continuous marketplace positioning;
- OCD—Organizational capital development, or continuous organizational alignment;
- HCD—Human capital development, or continuous human processing;
- ICD—Information capital development, or continuous information modeling;
- mCD—Mechanical capital development, or continuous mechanical tooling.

This related all capital development systems interdependently. Moreover, in the interdependent and synergistic processing between HCD and ICD, people would have to learn to process within the information models they had developed.

In short, Fisher and her group began to develop a phenomenal perspective of the possible:

- I^1 *Operational phenomena,*
- I^2 *Dimensional phenomena,*
- I^3 *Generative phenomena,*
- I^4 *Improved generative phenomena,*
- I^5 *Super-generative phenomena.*

Her group was now prepared for the interdependent processing of these interdependently related organizational phenomena.

INTERDEPENDENT PROCESSING SYSTEMS

Possibilities management is, finally, a science of phenomenal perspective. Perspective means being able to see phenomena in their various relationships. When our perspective becomes more expansive, we see more and more of the interdependent conditions within which an entity operates. We see relationships to larger and larger entities. When our perspective narrows, we see less and less context but more and more details. The details give us more information about the operations of our subject under study. We come to understand the performance measures, or *standards,* by which we operate.

For the possibilities manager, then, interdependent processing is about processing with phenomenal perspective. Operationally, this means gaining perspective on the phenomenon itself: its functions, components, and processes. It means expanding our perspective to understand the conditions within which phenomena operate: the conditions supply the answer to why the phenomena exist. Interdependent processing is about applying our processing technologies not only to the phenomena themselves, but also to their multiple contexts and the multiple performance measures by which they operate. Without perspective, we are lost in a *"micro-dot."* With perspective, we are empowered to see the phenomena for what they are and for what they might become.

Interdependent processing also means generating a perspective on the standards by which we measure our performance. These standards are a mix of the uniformity of current performance and the diversity of future performance. Each will change the other. Both will be measured on indices of changeability.

Interdependent processing is the culminating stage in possibilities management. After representing phenomenal images, the possibilities manager must develop images of the continuously changing conditions within which the phenomena operate, as well as images of the continuously changing standards that are generated within the phenomena (see Figure 6-5). The goal of interdependent processing, then, is to develop continuously changing perspectives of phenomenal possibilities. We do this by bringing our interpersonal and individual processing systems into interaction with the phenomenal systems that we have generated.

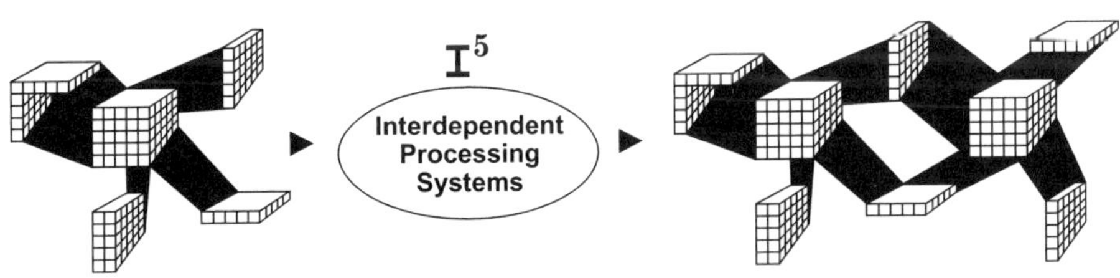

Figure 6-5. Interdependent Processing Systems

The Planning Leader

As general manager of the manufacturing division, Terry had great confidence in his leadership skills. With his relating skills, he could relate to the experiences of employees at all levels. With his representing skills, he could represent the dimensionality of any phenomena—people, data, things. With his individual processing skills, he could generate new images of productive operations. With his interpersonal processing skills, he could lead group processes—again, at all levels—to generate improved images of productive operations. His confidence came from these management skills.

Terry saw himself as an *"inclusive leader."* As such, he took everyone into consideration in developing policy. All that remained was a comprehensive planning system to accomplish the inclusively defined policy: mission, goals, objectives, programs, tasks, and so on. Planning systems were indelibly imprinted in his mind, as was the planning dictum *"Anything that can be defined can be planned and achieved."* Armed with the planning system, he could *control* outcomes by differentially reinforcing performance—administering rewards and punishments. Terry believed that planning and controlling were the real source of his leadership power. He was indeed *"The Planning Leader."*

Terry believed that he had a "lock" on the leadership paradigm:

Leadership = Relating + Planning + Controlling

A good model, right? Wrong! Terry soon discovered that this model could not keep pace with the spiraling changes of the marketplace—at all levels! Things were changing so rapidly that he could not include everyone. By the time a mission was planned, the conditions that influenced the original mission had changed. And control? Forget controlling anything! Control was impossible!

Terry believed that he had parts of the equation for leadership. He had the first part: relating inclusively. He had the last parts: planning and controlling. What he lacked were the parts in the middle: responses to the changing conditions—processing.

With study, Terry learned that he had hold of the twentieth-century model of management: relating, planning, controlling. This, he found, was an application of the paradigm for *the science of probabilities:*

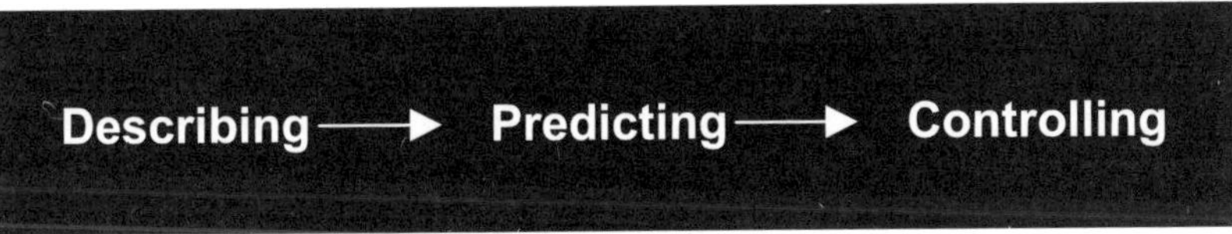

We relate to describe, plan to predict, and reinforce to control. Terry understood this was the paradigm that had given businesses such confidence in the twentieth century. He also saw that now, because of the rapidly changing conditions in the business environment, probabilities management no longer sufficed—indeed, by itself, it no longer worked!

What was needed was a *processing* paradigm rather than a planning paradigm. Terry discovered this need was fulfilled by a new paradigm for science and its applications—*the science of possibilities.*

He was impressed by the differences between the two sciences and their paradigms:

- Whereas probabilities science related externally to describe people and phenomena, possibilities science related internally to experience phenomena.
- Whereas probabilities planned to narrow the variability of phenomena, possibilities empowered to elevate the changeability of phenomena.
- Whereas probabilities controlled the performance of phenomena, possibilities freed the phenomena to become part of the change process.

These differences were clearly rooted in two contrasting assumptions:

- The probabilities paradigm assumed the relative stability of phenomena over time, and therefore sought to control them.
- The possibilities paradigm assumed the inherent changeability of phenomena, and therefore sought (1) to align with this change potential by relating, (2) to enhance the potential by empowering, and (3) to free that potential by releasing phenomena to seek their own changeable destinies. In short, the paradigm assumed that what you could not control, you aligned with.

Terry now reflected upon the changing customer requirements for the following:

- Continuous mechanical tooling and machining,
- Continuous information modeling and designing,
- Continuous human and information processing,
- Continuous organization aligning and architecture,
- Continuous positioning and partnering in the marketplace.

His conclusion was that only *the new science of possibilities* could address these requirements.

As a result of his discoveries, Terry emphasized the centrality of processing; that it must be ongoing and continuous; that it must be interdependent between all phenomena—evolving customers and organizations and employees as well as changing ideas, products, and services. He was determined to become *"The Processing Leader."*

Possibilities managers are both generative and innovative processors. They process inductively to generate new and powerful models of phenomena. They process deductively to innovate these models of phenomena.

The possibilities managers view the inductive and deductive processing systems in operation (see Figure 6-6). Note that the inductive processing systems culminate in generating new images of phenomena; in turn, the deductive processing systems culminate in innovating new images within, between, and among these images.

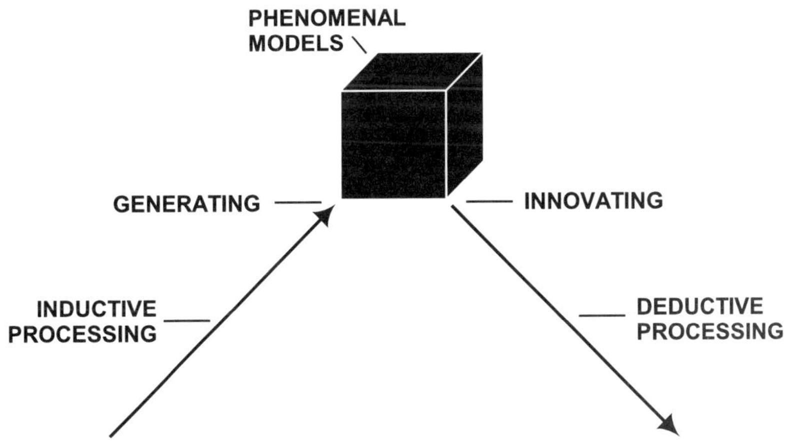

Figure 6-6. Inductive and Deductive Processing

The interactions of these inductive and deductive processes are the essence of possibilities science (see Figure 6-7). The results of each hypotheses-testing reflect back to innovate or modify the image of the phenomena: each test reflects a more accurate image of the phenomena; all tests move the phenomenal images toward convergence with the phenomena themselves. Thus, possibilities managers are continuously testing deductively to innovate prime phenomenal images.

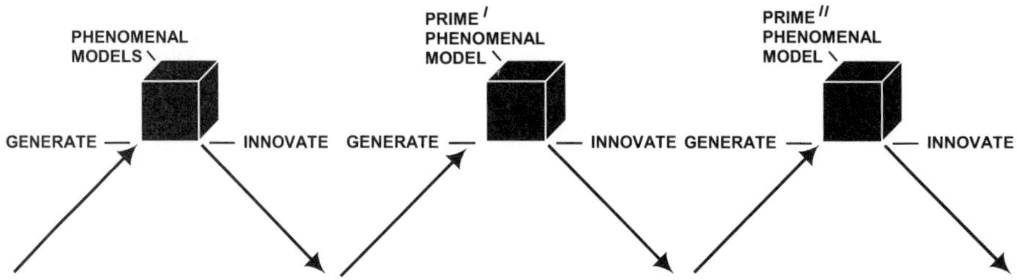

Figure 6-7. The Continuous Interactions of Inductive and Deductive Processing

For the possibilities manager, the inductive and deductive processes are clear (see Figure 6-8):

- The inductive processes *generate* new responses through interdependent processing systems—I^1, I^2, I^3, I^4, I^5.
- The deductive processes *innovate* new responses through interdependent processing systems—I^5, I^4, I^3, I^2, I^1.

While the inductive processes generate responses incrementally, the deductive processes innovate responses decrementally: only turning to lower-order systems upon realizing the limitations of higher-order systems; delivering lower-order systems to test hypotheses in support of building responses in higher-order systems.

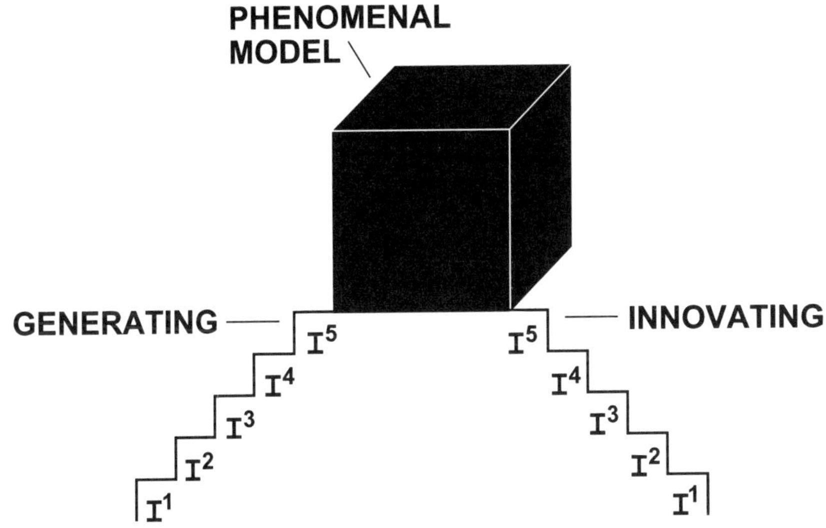

Figure 6-8. Inductive and Deductive Processing

In their full complexity, the possibilities managers are processing inductively with three qualitatively different human processing systems (see Figure 6-9):

- Stimulus-response (S-R) conditioned responding systems, which define the operations of the conditioned responses;
- Stimulus-organism-response (S-O-R) discriminative learning systems, which represent or model dimensional images to replace the operational images of phenomena;
- Stimulus-processor-response (S-P-R) generative processing systems, which generate increasingly more powerful images of phenomena.

At the highest levels of the S-P-R systems, the inductive processors are processing with different phenomenal processing systems, such as the organizational (S-OP-R) processing systems. These phenomenal processing systems enable the processors to generate the phenomenal models.

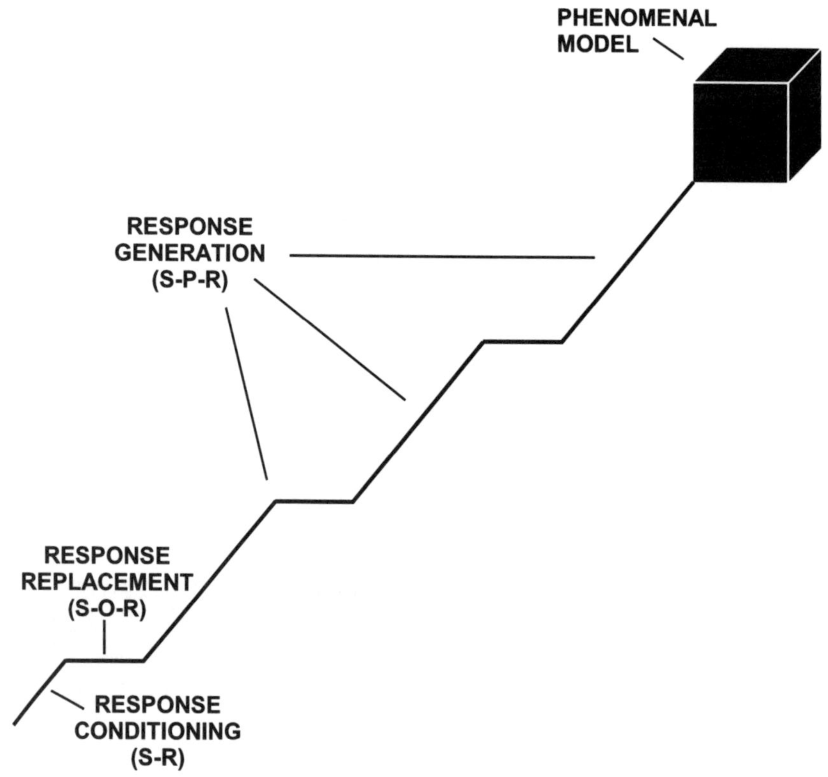

Figure 6-9. The Processing Systems of Inductive Processing

Deductively, the possibilities managers are also processing with these qualitatively different human processing systems (see Figure 6-10):

- S-P-R generative processing systems, which empower them to innovate within the phenomenal models;
- S-O-R discriminative learning systems, which enable them to innovate response-replacement images of the phenomenal models;
- S-R conditioned responding systems, which enable them to innovate new conditioned response operations.

Again, the S-P-R systems process interdependently with phenomenal processing systems to generate improved images of the phenomenal models.

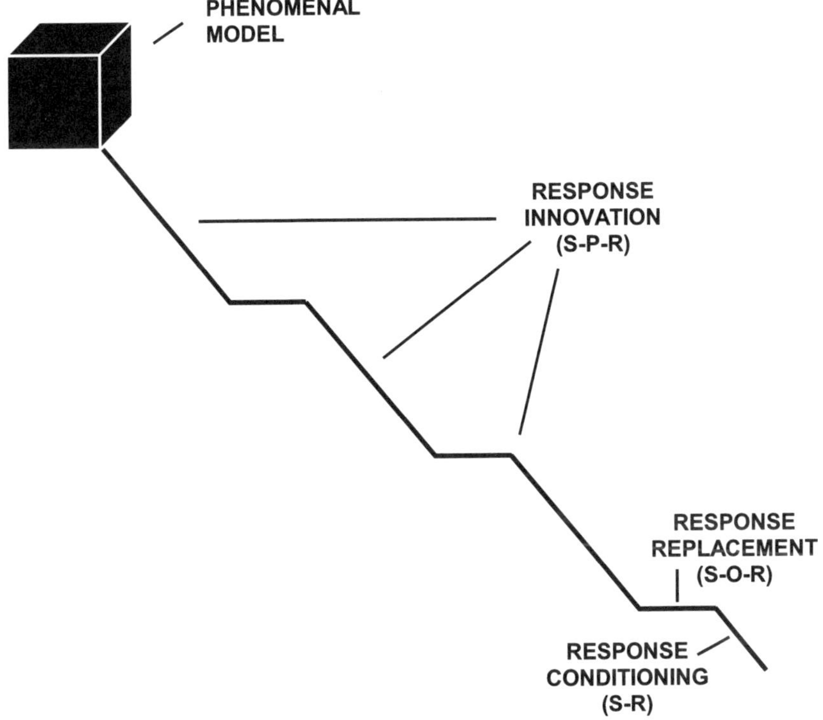

Figure 6-10. The Processing Systems of Deductive Processing

Inclusively, the possibilities managers process interactively with all human processing systems (see Figure 6-11):

- Inductively building models by building responses;
- Deductively testing hypotheses for response performance;
- Interactively improving the images of the phenomenal models.

Interdependent phenomenal processing is a continuous and life-long process: continuous because the phenomena are constantly changing; life-long because the changes extend eternally to the lives of the phenomena and the processors.

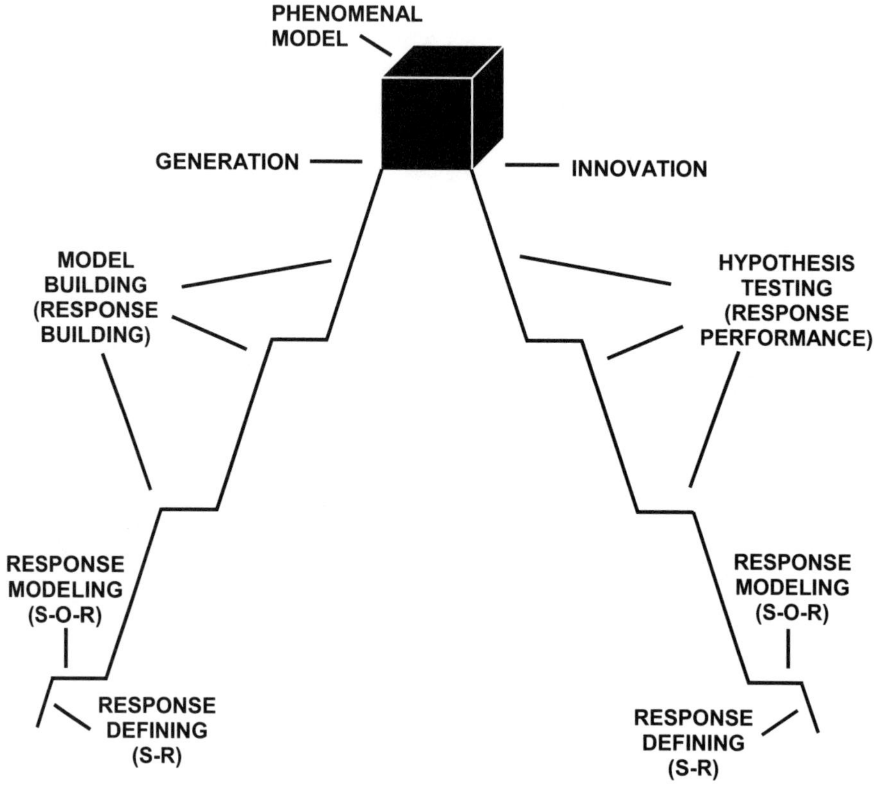

Figure 6-11. The Model Building and Hypothesis-Testing of Inductive and Deductive Processing

The interdependent phenomenal processing systems enable the possibilities managers to process continuously with constantly evolving phenomena.

Inductive Generating

The essence of interdependent processing is to generate phenomenal models and then process within these phenomenal worlds. Let us select one very difficult phenomenon to process: the societal system required for full participation in the twenty-first-century global economy. Let us develop images of this phenomenon inductively and, then, live inside these images to refine the phenomenon.

In this context, we can initiate phenomenal modeling by scaling phenomenal dimensions with which we are quite familiar: those for governance. Table 6-1, below, illustrates governance using a simple linear scale of phenomenal functions.

Table 6-1. Scale for Governance

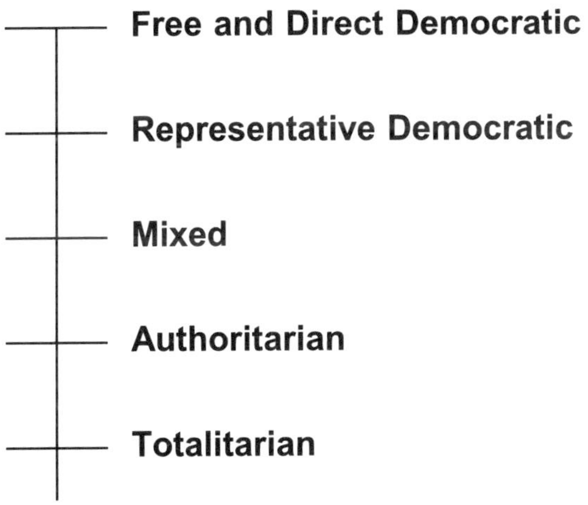

- Free and Direct Democratic
- Representative Democratic
- Mixed
- Authoritarian
- Totalitarian

As shown, the scales range from direct and representative democratic governance to authoritarian and totalitarian governance. In terms of the meaning of societal requirements for the twenty-first-century global community, most people would agree that the higher levels of free democratic governance will contribute to full participation. However, most people would view governance in relation to supporting economic functions.

Relatedly, we may continue phenomenal modeling with the scaling of economic dimensions, as shown in Table 6-2. As may be noted, the levels of economic functions range from free-enterprise and capitalistic economies to command and control economics. As may also be noted, the governance dimension has been rotated inductively, or clockwise, to become components in a matrix dedicated to accomplishing economic functions.

Table 6-2. Economic Matrix

ECONOMIC FUNCTIONS \ GOVERNANCE COMPONENTS	Free Democratic	Representative	Mixed	Authoritarian	Totalitarian
Free Enterprise					
Capitalism					
Mixed					
Command					
Control					

Again, most people would concur with the results of our processing, and agree that these dimensions are requirements for participation in the global marketplace. We may define the mission of the economic matrix as follows:

Free-enterprise-driven economic functions are discharged by free democratic-driven governance components.

In this context, we may continue phenomenal modeling with the scaling of cultural dimensions (see Figure 6-12). Here the levels of cultural dimensions range from interdependent through independent to dependent. Note that the economic and governance dimensions have been rotated inductively, or clockwise: the economic dimensions have become components dedicated to accomplishing cultural functions; the governance dimensions have become processes enabling the economic components to discharge cultural functions.

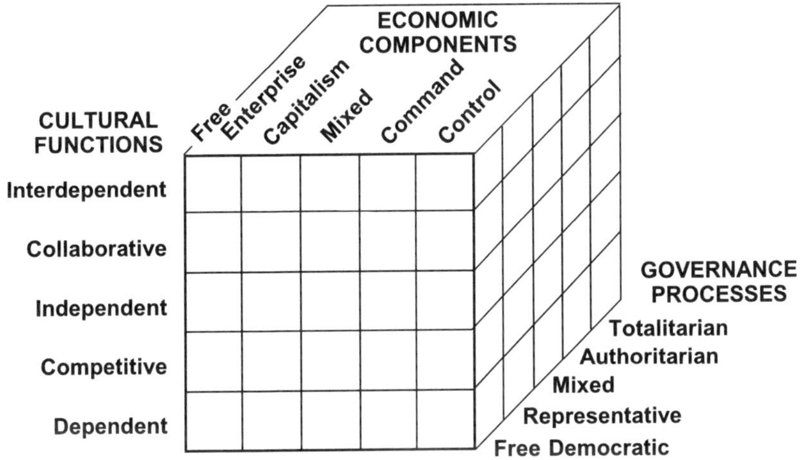

Figure 6-12. The Cultural Capital Development Model

Most people would agree that the model we have constructed from these dimensions fits the global requirements of the twenty-first century. We call this model the cultural capital development (CCD) model and define its mission as follows:

> *Interdependency-driven cultural functions are discharged by free-enterprise-driven economic components enabled by free democratic-driven governance processes.*

This illustration of inductive generativity serves two fundamental purposes:

1. It demonstrates that we can generate the most complex of models—in this case, a CCD model for addressing twenty-first-century global requirements.

2. It enables us to fully enter the experience of CCD, to become *"one"* with its cultural functions, economic components, and governance processes.

Thus, the CCD experience lives for us: we are able to process interdependently within, between, and among its dimensions.

We now have a model that will help us meet our twenty-first-century global requirements. We may employ it to generate testable models within which we can innovate. In order to do this, we must model deductively.

Deductive Innovation

When we model deductively, we rotate dimensions counter-clockwise to incorporate the enabling processes. In this case, we rotate our economic dimensions to become driving functions and our governance dimensions to become components dedicated to discharging the functions. Then we ask the question *"What processes will it take to enable these governance components to accomplish these economic functions?"* In this instance, we have answered with new capital development (NCD) processing systems:

- **MCD**—Marketplace capital development through corporate positioning in the marketplace;
- **OCD**—Organizational capital development through organizational alignment with corporate positioning;
- **HCD**—Human capital development through human processing to implement organizational alignment;
- **ICD**—Information capital development through information modeling to enable human processing;
- **mCD**—Mechanical capital development through mechanical tooling to implement information modeling.

The result is shown in Figure 6-13.

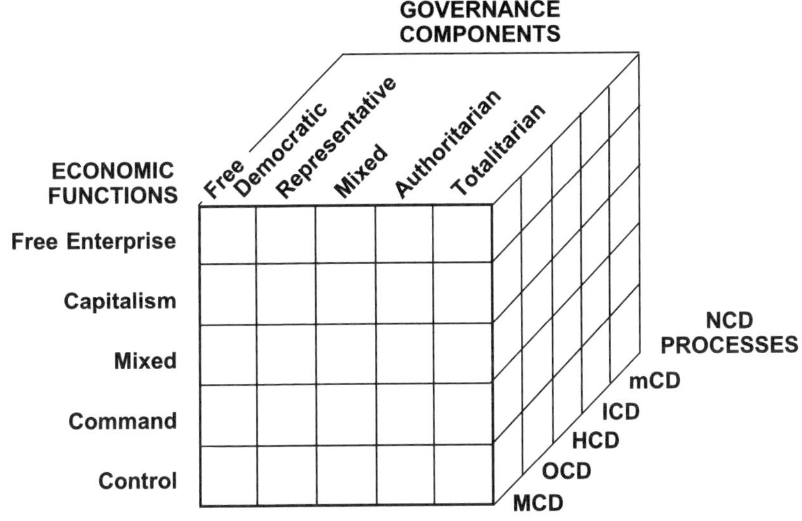

Figure 6-13. The Economic Capital Development Model

Once again, most people would agree with the result of our processing—in this case, the economic capital development model. We simply need to develop new sources of capital in order to enable governance processes to discharge economic functions. We may now define the mission of the economic capital development (ECD) model:

> *Free-enterprise-driven economic functions are discharged by free democratic-driven governance components enabled by NCD processing systems.*

In the illustrations that follow, the NCD processing systems are deductively modeled.

MCD

In the marketplace capital development model (Figure 6-14), the MCD functions, components, and processes are identified. The functions of MCD are derived from the market's requirements for NCD systems: MCD, OCD, HCD, ICD, and mCD. Essentially, the marketplace of organizations is dedicated to fulfilling these NCD requirements. The MCD components are the corporate technologies available among organizations in the marketplace: MT, OT, HT, IT, mT. These technologies are critical to fulfilling the requirements of the marketplace. The processes of the MCD model are organizational processing systems: leadership, marketing, resources, technology, production. To summarize:

> *Marketplace technologies are dedicated to new capital development enabled by organizational processing systems.*

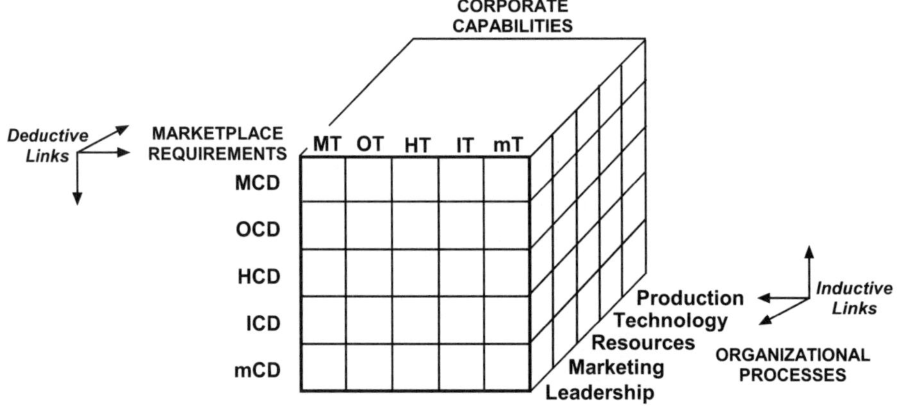

Figure 6-14. Marketplace Capital Development Model

The relationships of these marketplace requirements, technological capabilities, and organizational processing systems define MCD. The interaction of these dimensions defines MCD alignment. Once we realize the interrelational nature of MCD, we may link these dimensions with intentionality, doing so deductively, inductively, or functionally.

OCD

The functions of OCD are derived from the market's technology requirements (see Figure 6-15). These requirements are translated operationally into functional levels of the organization: policy, executive, management, supervision, and delivery. Essentially, the resources of the organization will be dedicated to fulfilling these marketplace requirements. The OCD components are units of the organization and are derived from the processes of the MCD model: leadership, marketing, resources (and their integration), technology, and production. These organizational units are critical to fulfilling market requirements. The processes of the OCD model are introduced as HCD processes: goaling, inputting, processing, planning, outputting. These HCD processes are essential for organizations to fulfill their goals. To summarize:

> *OCD components are dedicated to MCD functions enabled by HCD processing systems.*

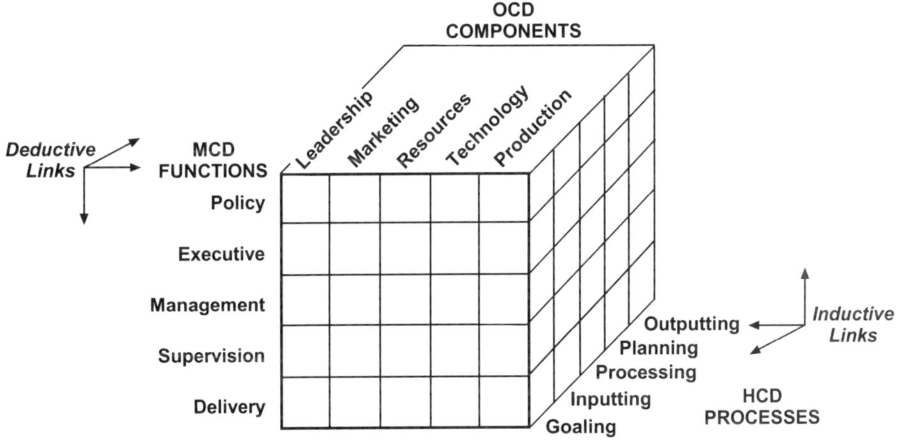

Figure 6-15. Organizational Capital Development Model

HCD

In the human capital development (HCD) model, OCD components have been rotated to become the functions of HCD: leadership, marketing, resources, technology, production (see Figure 6-16). Human capital is thus dedicated to fulfilling these organizational goals. Similarly, the HCD processes of the OCD model have been rotated to become HCD components: goaling, inputting, processing, planning, outputting. These human processing components are critical to fulfilling the goals of the organization. Finally, the information capital development (ICD) processes by which the HCD components discharge OCD functions are introduced: phenomenal, vectorial, dimensional, operational, and conceptual. These ICD processes are essential for human processing. Note that each lower-order ingredient is dedicated to enabling the achievement of a higher-order function:

> *HCD components are dedicated to OCD functions and enabled by ICD processes.*

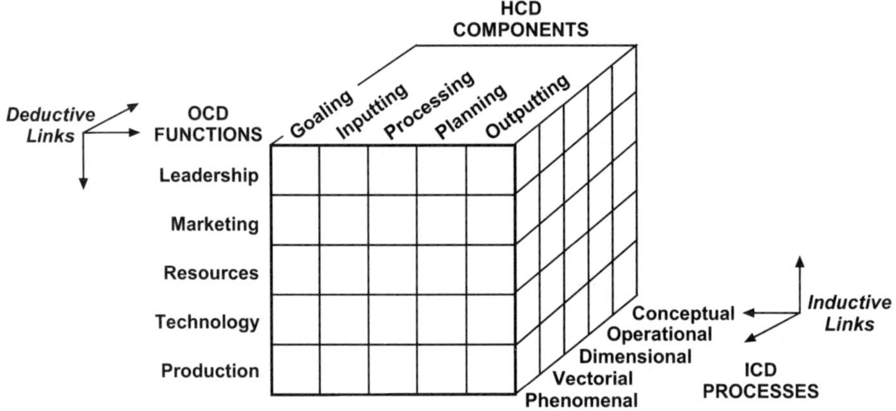

Figure 6-16. Human Capital Development Model

These relationships of OCD functions, HCD components, and ICD processes define HCD. The interaction of these dimensions defines HCD alignment. Once we realize the interrelational nature of HCD, we may link its dimensions with intentionality, doing so deductively, inductively, or functionally.

ICD

In the ICD model, HCD components have been rotated to become the functions of ICD; in other words, information capital is dedicated to servicing the requirements of thinking people (see Figure 6-17). Likewise, the ICD processes of the HCD model have been rotated to become ICD components. These information components are critical ingredients in the service of human processing. Finally, mCD operations are introduced as enabling operationalizing processes: functions, components, processes, conditions, standards. These mechanical operations are essential to information-capital processing. Again, note that the lower-order ingredients are dedicated to achieving higher-order functions:

> *ICD components service HCD goals by way of mCD processes.*

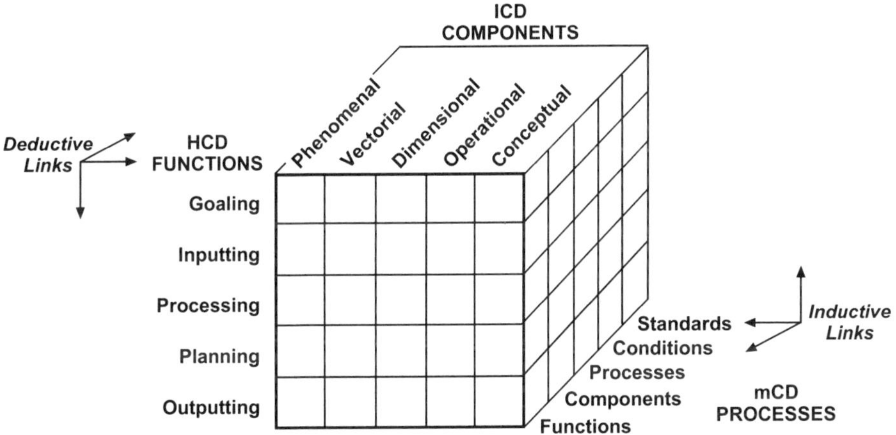

Figure 6-17. Information Capital Development Model

These interactions of HCD functions, ICD components, and mCD processes define ICD and its alignment. We may now link these dimensions with intentionality as well, deductively, inductively, or functionally.

mCD

The mechanical capital development model has ICD components that have been rotated to become the functions of mCD (see Figure 6-18). Mechanical capital, or mechanical tools, are dedicated to servicing information designs (ICD). In turn, the mCD processes of the ICD model have been rotated to become mCD components. These mechanical components are critical to fulfilling information designs. Finally, new mCD′ programming processes are introduced: programs, instructions, tasks, steps, implementation. These programmatic mechanical processes are essential to mechanical processing. Again, lower-order ingredients are dedicated to higher-order functions:

> *mCD components service ICD functions by way of mCD′ processes.*

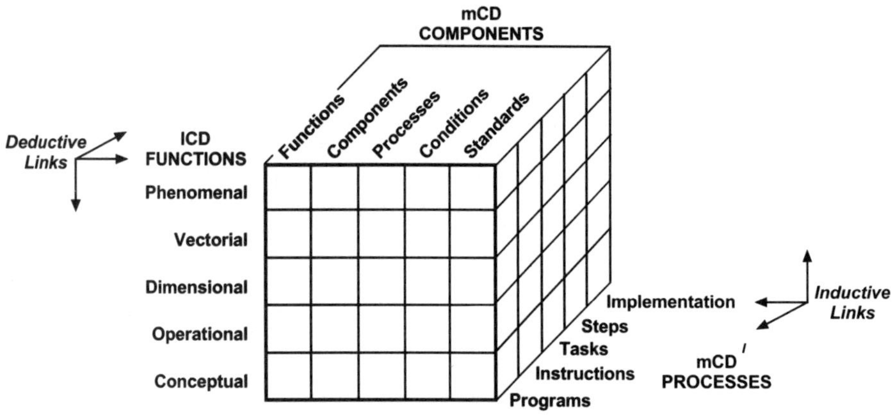

Figure 6-18. Mechanical Capital Development Model

The interaction of these dimensions and their relationships defines mCD and its alignment. We may now also link these dimensions with intentionality, doing so deductively, inductively, or functionally.

In interdependent processing, then, we may process inside any cell of our phenomenal models. For example, we may begin with the first cell in our organizational model, the leadership unit: policy-making (or positioning) functions are discharged by leadership-driven components enabled by goaling-driven processes. Here we may pull down a screen for organizational positioning in the marketplace: corporate capacities in technologies dedicated to marketplace requirements (see Figure 6-19). We may begin by mapping ourselves into our organization's current marketplace positioning:

> *Information technologies (IT) dedicated to ICD functions.*

In this instance, our data management systems are dedicated to fulfilling ICD functions.

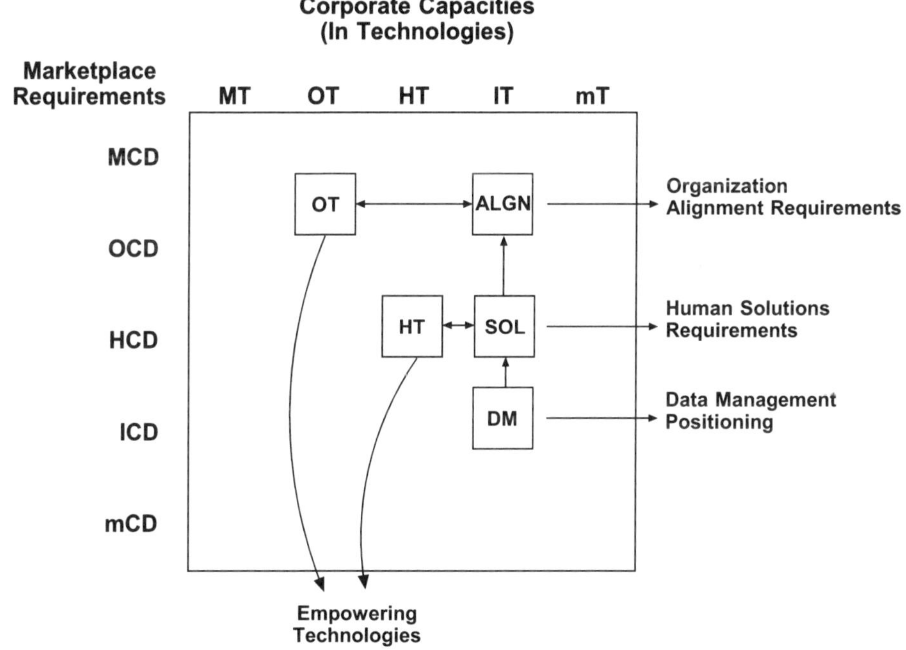

Figure 6-19. MCD Positioning in the Marketplace

Interdependent processing means that we become *"one"* with the phenomenon: positioning our organization as a developer and purveyor of data management systems. When we process interdependently with the marketplace requirements, we discover that customers are asking for more than data management. They are asking for information capital management at higher and higher levels:

- Conceptual,
- Operational,
- Dimensional,
- Vectorial,
- Phenomenal.

In other words, they are requiring all levels of ICD.

As we elevate our data management systems, we begin to understand the need for technologies to address higher-level functions:

- Human solutions regarding data management,
- Organizational alignment regarding data management.

This means that we require the empowering technologies to address these functional levels:

- Human processing technologies to address human solutions,
- Organizational alignment technologies to address organizational alignment issues.

Perhaps we will consider interdependent partnerships to empower ourselves and our partners in the necessary technologies. In any event, we engage in continuous interdependent processing to achieve or change our marketplace positioning.

The Processing Leader

Terry's great insight into interdependent processing was this: *we live in the house that we build!* After we have related to merge with phenomena and have represented multidimensional images of phenomena, then we process these phenomena to generate the most productive and growthful images of the phenomena; after all this preparation and processing, we must learn to process for and with the phenomena themselves—to process with the phenomena we have just constructed.

For Terry, this meant that he and his processing team would process for and with the marketplace in seeking to position their corporation. It was clear to Terry and his team that their corporation was positioned to address mechanical capital development (mCD) requirements and, increasingly, information capital development (ICD) requirements.

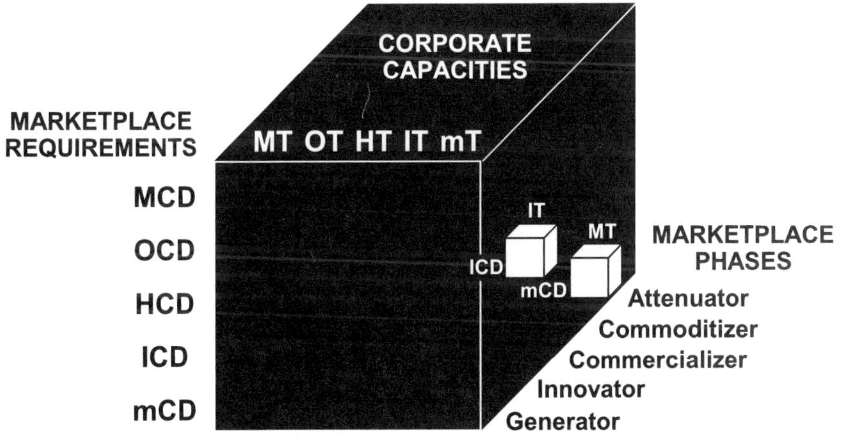

The processing team processed interdependently with the appropriate cells. They discovered that although the corporation had special expertise in mechanical technologies (mT) and, increasingly, information technologies (IT), and was superior in addressing mCD requirements, it was inadequate in meeting

ICD requirements. Indeed, neither they nor anyone in the IT business really knew what ICD was! Unless they built this capacity, they could not market themselves in the ICD marketplace.

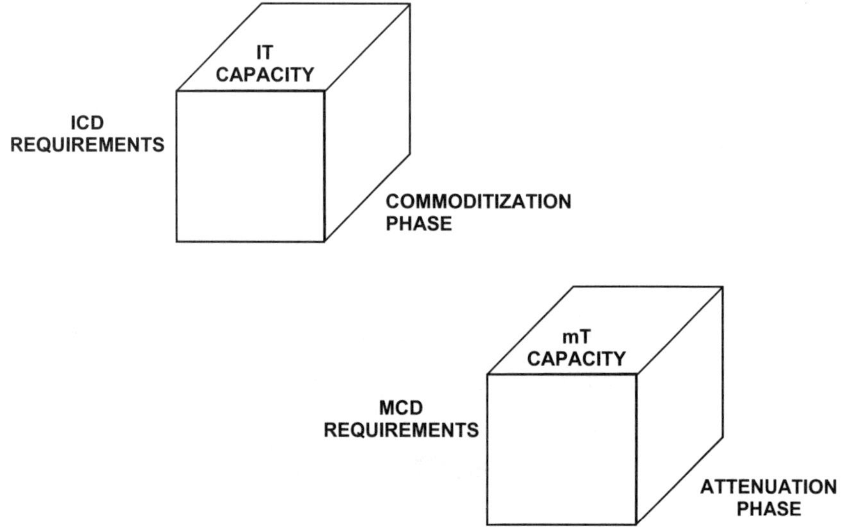

The positioning team also realized the implications of their choices concerning marketplace positioning. The mechanical technologies had crested as a source of comparative advantage in the early 1960s, at the height of the Industrial Age. While manufacturing was still a huge market, the playing field was level for foreign as well as American competitors. They were in the attenuation phase of the market curve.

This meant that anyone could play who was willing to pay: investment of great resources promised diminishing returns. In turn, while the information technologies had defined the Data Age, they had peaked as a source of comparative advantage in the 1980s. They were in the commoditization phase of the curve. The innovation-competition curve had accelerated so that the competitive edge lasted anywhere from six months to two years. Investing now meant modest returns.

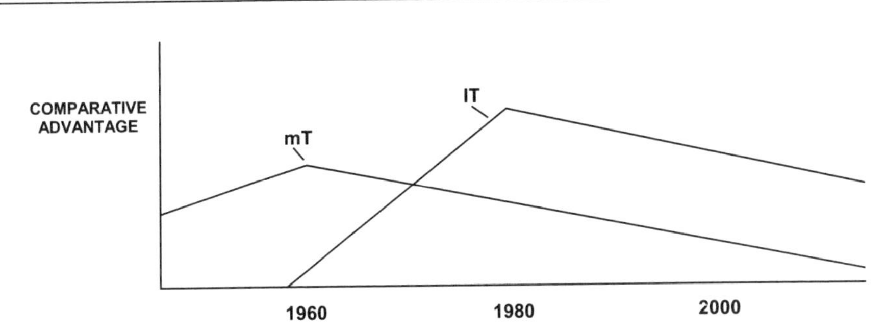

Nevertheless, the processing team was driven by values emphasizing mechanical technological expertise: *"Stick to what we're good at!"* Moreover, they believed that they could become an innovative corporation within the attenuation market. As for their interest in addressing ICD markets in the future, they believed that they could at least get even with the commoditizer phase by adopting *"best practices."*

They integrated their positioning in the marketplace: meeting mCD and ICD requirements with mT and IT capacities in attenuator and commoditizer markets.

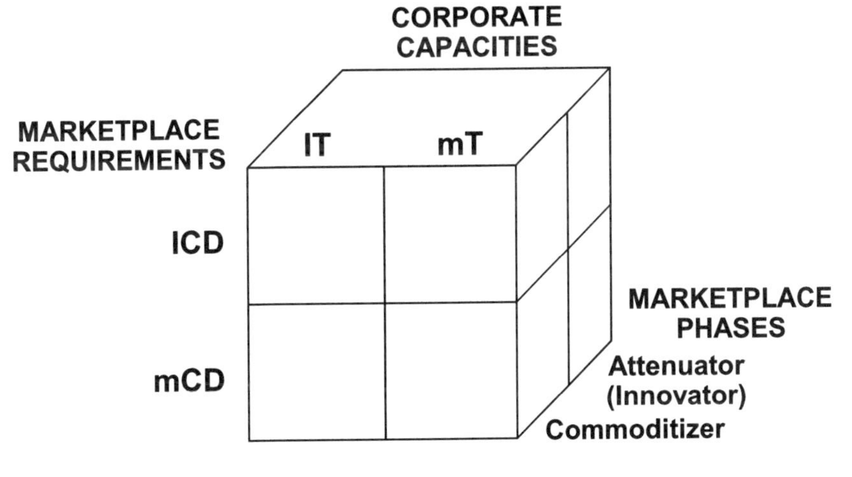

The focus of Terry's processing team now shifted to the alignment of the organization to implement this positioning. The team modeled the organization accordingly. In general, the functions in such a model are derived from positioning:

- Policymakers represent marketplace positioning;
- Executives "architect" the organizational alignment;
- Managers design the systems to achieve the alignment goals;
- Delivery people and team members perform the tasks to achieve the objectives.

The organization is dedicated to accomplishing these functions derived from marketplace positioning.

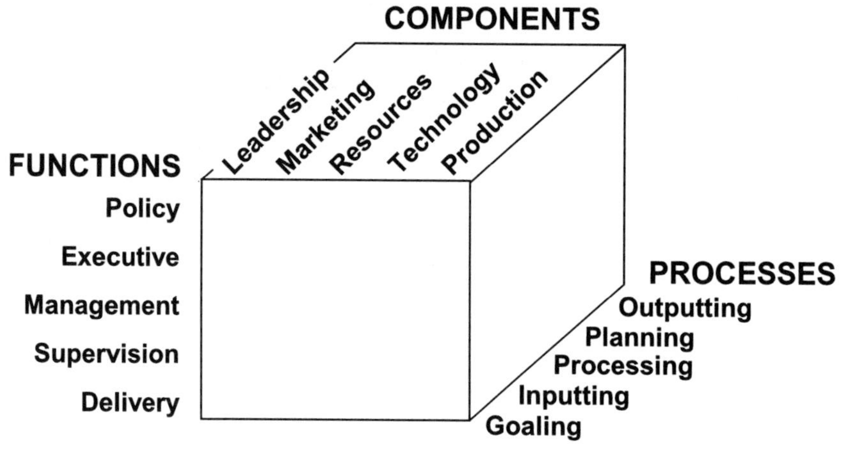

In turn, the components of the organization are dedicated to discharging or accomplishing the functions. The components themselves have continuously changing meaning. Basically, they are derived from the marketplace processes:

- The leadership component represents generativity in marketplace processing by generating initiatives in the marketplace;

- The marketing component represents innovativeness in marketplace processing by eliciting input concerning customer needs;
- The resources, or resource-integration, component represents commercialization in marketplace processing by tailoring products and services to customer needs;
- The technology component represents commoditization in processing by customizing products and services;
- The production component represents attenuation in processing by standardizing products and services.

Again, the components enable us to accomplish our functions.

Finally, the organizational processes are introduced. Basically, the processes enable the components to discharge the functions. The phases of organizational processing are familiar to anyone who has ever participated in an organization:

- Goaling, or establishing values;
- Inputting, or eliciting data;
- Processing, or generating information;
- Planning, or modeling information;
- Outputting, or producing products.

Again, the organizational processes enable the components to discharge their functions.

Terry's processing team now mapped themselves into the policymaking function. In interpersonal processing, they had expanded the organizational components dedicated to the policymaking functions to include the following: leadership, marketing, resources, technology, and production.

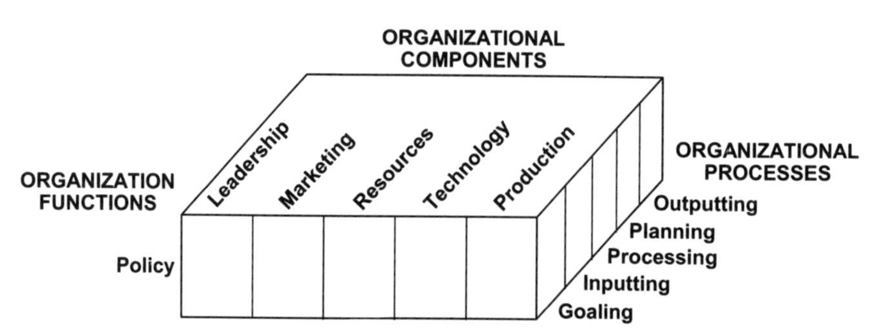

The processing team rotated the model to focus upon the organizational processes needed for the components to discharge policymaking functions: goaling, inputting, processing, planning, outputting. This would enable them to penetrate the processing within every unit of the organization.

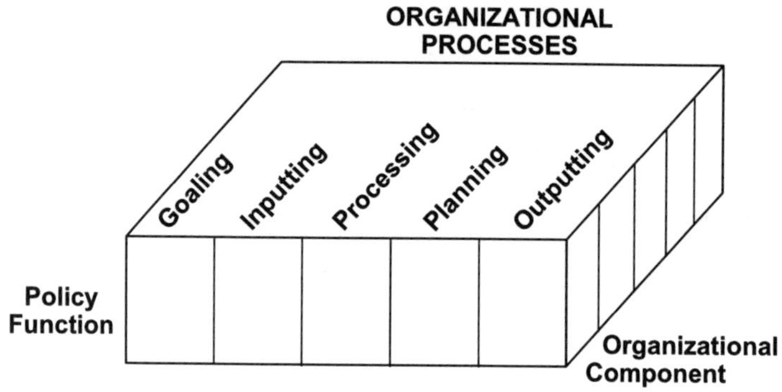

When the processing team penetrated any of the cells within organizational processes, they found that human processing emphasized all of the phases leading up to interdependent processing:

- I^1—Information relating systems,
- I^2—Information representing systems,
- I^3—Individual processing systems,
- I^4—Interpersonal processing systems,
- I^5—Interdependent processing systems.

They realized that interdependent processing had to occur within every unit and cell of an organization.

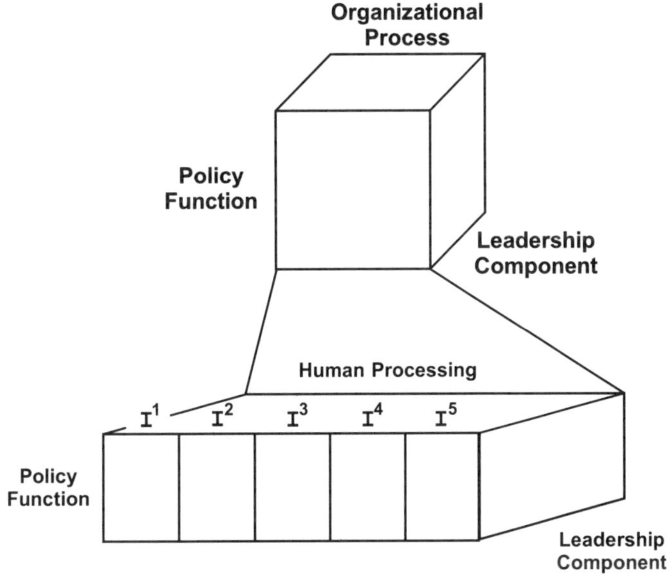

Finally, Terry's processing team discovered the meaning of the elusive information capital development systems. By penetrating the information representing system, or I^2, they discovered the differentiated levels of ICD:

- Conceptual information, or verbal statements of relationships between phenomena;
- Operational information, or operational definitions of phenomena;
- Dimensional information, or multidimensional models of phenomena;
- Vectorial information, or expert-driven models of vectorial systems;
- Phenomenal information, or continuously changing and interdependently related, multidimensional and curvi-

linear information about phenomena as they exist in their natural states.

The team resolved that ICD would be addressed at all levels of their operations.

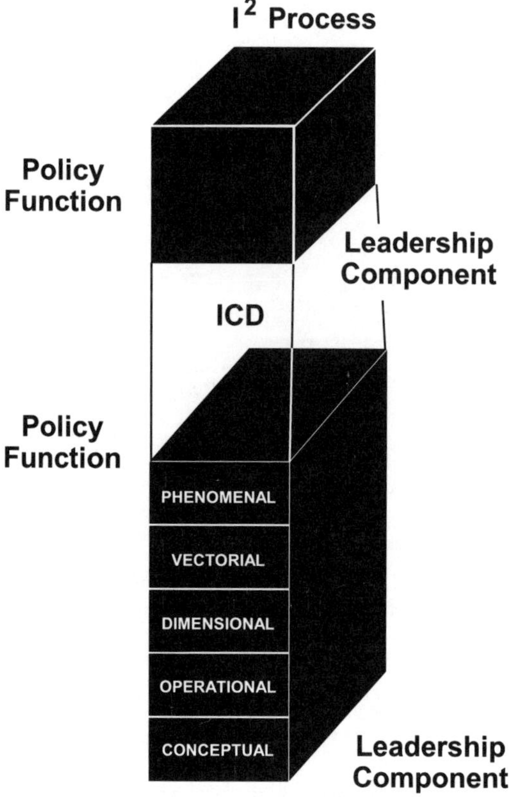

Terry and his processing team were ecstatic with their own performance. They had processed generatively, both individually and interpersonally, and had *nested* this processing within the organizational phenomena they had generated. As a result, their corporate mission had been accomplished. They had processed with and within all of the following:

- Corporate positioning in the marketplace (we label this positioning "marketplace capital development," or "MCD");
- Organizational alignment with that positioning (we label this alignment "organizational capital development," or "OCD");
- Human processing in that alignment (we term this processing "human capital development," or "HCD");
- Information modeling to support human processing (we term this modeling "information capital development," or "ICD");
- Mechanical tooling to implement information modeling (we label this tooling "mechanical capital development," or "mCD").

Moreover, they had positioned the organization for future, continuous processing of these capital development functions.

As far as Terry was concerned, he had defined leadership in the twenty-first century:

Leadership = Continuous Interdependent Processing

Put another way:

Leadership = I^5

In Transition

The threshold phase of new capital development is human capital development, or HCD. The I^5 interdependent processing systems that we are studying are the core of this HCD. The I^5 systems empower us to receive the goals and input, to generate new and more productive ways of accomplishing them, and then to plan and output them. With HCD, all new capital development is possible! Without HCD, nothing is possible!

A valuable tool for managing I^5 is provided in Table 6-3. With this tool, we may assess our employees' levels of preparation for interdependent processing of different phenomena:

1. *Have they defined and dimensionalized the functions of the phenomena?*
2. *Have they defined and dimensionalized the components of the phenomena?*
3. *Have they defined and dimensionalized the processes of the phenomena?*
4. *Have they defined and dimensionalized the conditions within which the phenomena operate?*
    - *Marketplace conditions? Organizational conditions? Human conditions? Information conditions? Mechanical conditions?*
5. *Have they defined and dimensionalized the standards of performance by which the phenomena operate?*
    - *Marketplace standards? Organizational standards? Human standards? Information standards? Mechanical standards?*

Table 6-3. I^5 Management Systems

LEVELS OF I^5	Marketplace	Organization	Human	Information	Mechanical
5. Standards					
4. Conditions					
3. Processes					
2. Components					
1. Functions					

(Column heading: AREAS OF PHENOMENA)

The answers to these questions will dictate our level of confidence in our employees as well as in the phenomena.

Case: The Possibilities Leader (concluded)

Again, Fisher and her colleagues were excited about their discoveries. They found that interdependent processing applications also can take many unique forms, depending upon the unique interactions of the phenomenal processing with the interpersonal processing. For instance, further generative interdependent processing resulted in images of partnered possibilities organizations such as those shown in Figure 6-20. Here the partnered organizations share both marketing components and delivery functions. Because they address the same marketplace with the same issues, the partners process interdependently within the marketing component. Because the partners also have the same delivery functions, they process interdependently to deliver products and services.

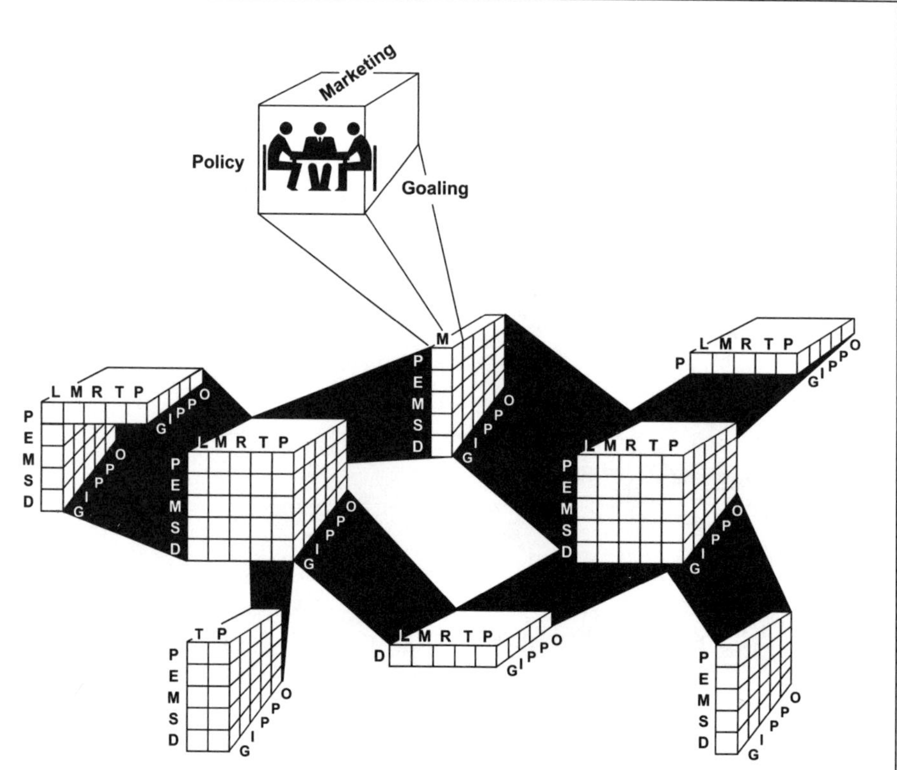

Figure 6-20. Partnered Possibilities Organizations

As detailed in Figure 6-21, the interdependent processing teams are *nested* within each of the units. In our illustration, the partnered processing teams are engaged in interdependent processing within the following cell: *marketing components discharging policymaking functions through goaling.* As may be noted, the processing teams are processing for the organizational unit by considering marketplace requirements and organizational capacity. The teams process interdependently with this positioning matrix to position the company to meet ICD and mCD requirements with IT and mT corporate capacities.

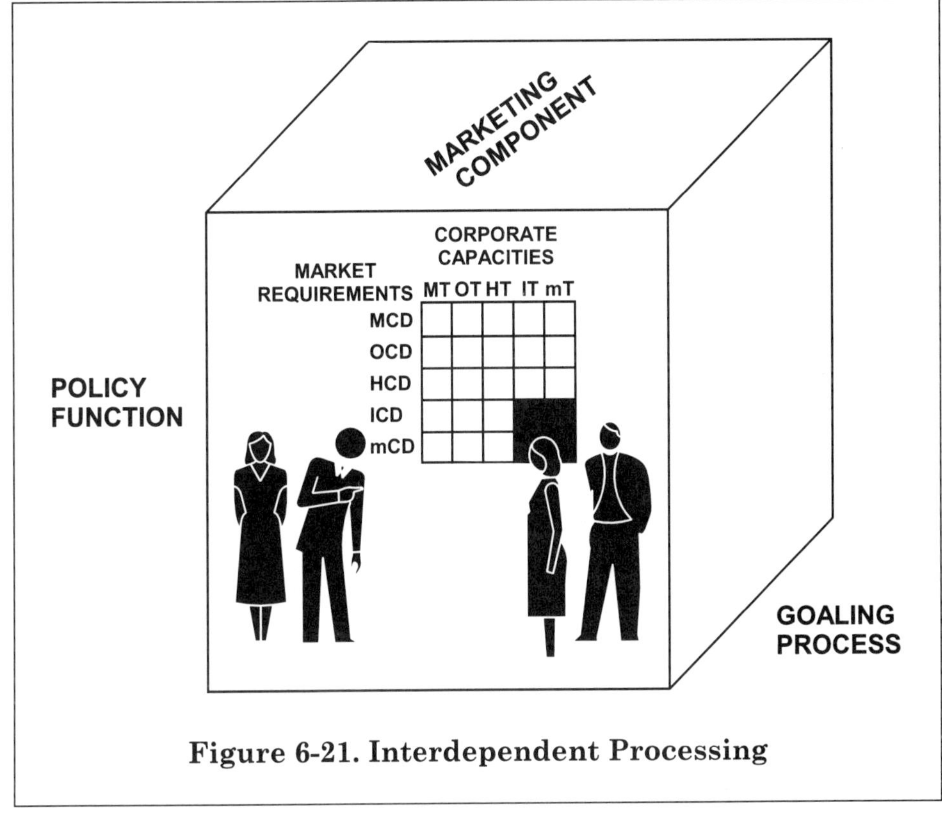

Figure 6-21. Interdependent Processing

We are now only beginning to get an image of the most complex of all processing: interdependent phenomenal processing. For example, we may select the most leveraged cell in the most complex phenomena we have illustrated (see Figure 6-22): interdependent cultural-relating functions discharged by free-enterprise economic components enabled by free and direct democratic governance processes. Note that, overall, our movement in the twenty-first century is away from controlling and toward freeing.

Note, too, that we have also generated the models for conditions from which our new capital development (NCD) systems may be generated. By further rotating the model for societal standards deductively, or counterclockwise, we derive our model for MCD, or

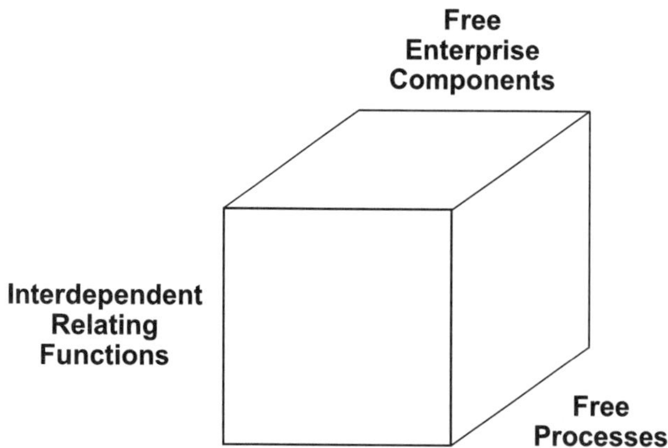

Figure 6-22. The Model for Leveraged Participation in the Global Economy

marketplace positioning—NCD requirements are achieved by corporate technological capacities empowered by organizational processes—and so on, for OCD, HCD, ICD, mCD.

We have now generated models for one of the most complex of all phenomena: the societal system for participating fully in the twenty-first century global marketplace. We have represented a model for *"a free and empowered society."* We have articulated the society's dimensions and scaled them. It remains for us to engage in the processing necessary to achieve those dimensions: continuous interdependent phenomenal processing. Interdependent processing is the source of all possibilities!

Most important, whether our models are generated inductively or deductively, we are going to learn to live within them and process their dimensions:

- Function outputs that represent the purposes of the phenomena;
- Component inputs that are dedicated to accomplishing the functions;
- Processes that enable the components to discharge the functions;

- Conditions that define the contexts within which these processes take place;
- Standards that measure the level of achievement of our processing systems.

We will become *"one"* with the phenomena. We will process interdependently within, between, and among phenomena.

In summary, the purpose of interdependent processing is to relate interdependently to phenomenal operations, including their conditions and their standards of performance. As possibilities leaders often say, *"We become* ***one*** *with the phenomena, but more than that, we become* ***multiple*** *with their changing phenomenal experiences."*

Everything is interdependently related to everything else, and all things—including ourselves—are changeable. This is the basic principle of interdependent processing: ***everything is interdependent and changeable.*** Are we willing to elevate our processes to relate to our changing, interdependent world?

In transition, we prepare for interdependent processing by relating to phenomena and representing them. We initiate interdependent processing by processing individually and interpersonally within the phenomena. However, we do not culminate interdependent processing until we become the phenomena themselves and process with their systems (see Figure 6-23). Again, *we live in the house that we built! And we—and they—keep changing it!*

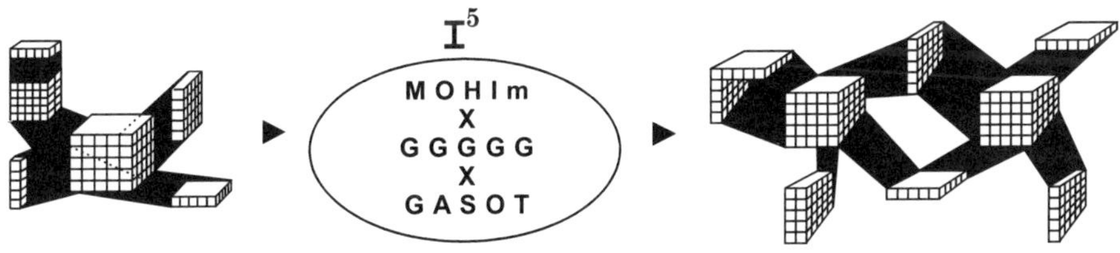

Figure 6-23. Interdependent Processing Systems

III

Summary and Transition

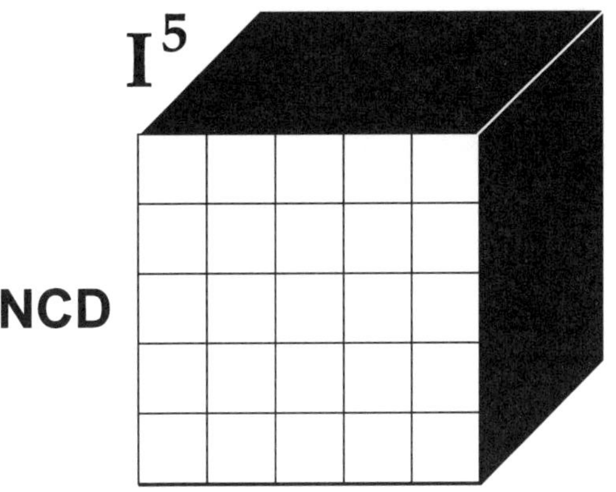

7 Process-Centric Change

$I^5 \longleftrightarrow$ NCD

The issue of transforming people from planners to processors is an issue of individual change. Humankind resists change and accepts it only reluctantly. Individual change is akin to therapeutic personality change: where we were closed, we are now open; where we were comfortable, we are now growing; where we were independent of our daily tasks, we are now *"interdependently one."*

The goal of individual change is freedom for initiating both entrepreneurally and intrapreneurally. This freedom is expressed in the multiplication of quantity and the elevation of quality of responses.

The vehicle to individual change is empowerment. By discovering exemplary possibilities performers, we define the curriculum of change. The starting point is relating. We relate to our change candidates from their internal frames of reference.

These factors are the fundamental principles of the new science of possibilities:

- Relating to define the change candidates' potential;
- Empowering to enhance the candidates' potential;
- Freeing to release the candidates' potential.

With possibilities science, we get what we process. And it's usually a lot more than we would have predicted.

These possibilistic factors contrast vividly with those of the old science of probabilities:

- Describing the change candidates' current performance;
- Predicting the candidates' future performance;
- Controlling the candidates' future performance.

With probabilities science, we get exactly what we plan for. No more! No less!

We may view the probabilistic performance of change candidates in Figure 7-1. As shown, a moderate level of performance elicits predictions of similar performance over time. We then control the performance in order to validate our expectancies. In short, we get what we plan for—and it is not a happy state.

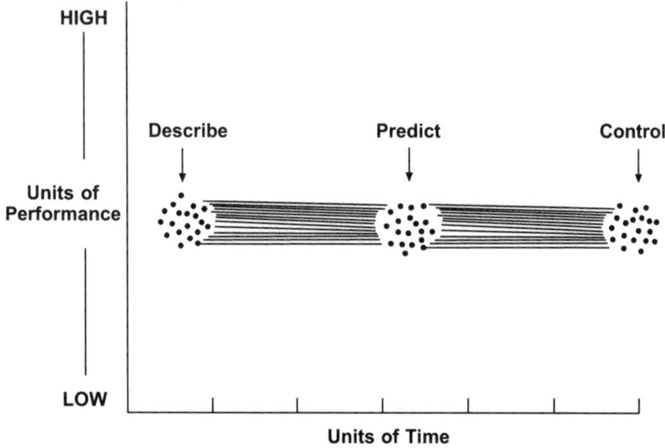

Figure 7-1. Probabilistic Performance

We may view the possibilistic performance of change candidates in Figure 7-2. As may be noted, a moderate level of performance is transformed to a higher level by an empowerment experience. With their empowerment, the candidates are then released to express their full and changing potential. For example, they may begin to define the work experience from tasks to missions, all the time keeping goals of growth in performance, productivity, and profit.

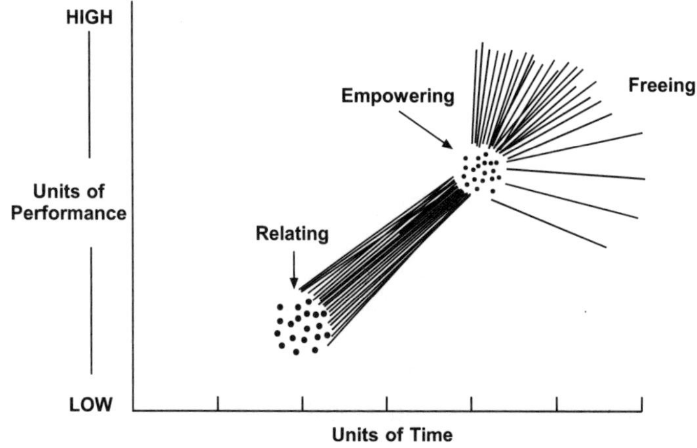

Figure 7-2. Possibilistic Performance

It is interesting to note that the source of empowerment first narrows the variability of performance before expanding its diversity and changeability. That is because we are employing probabilities methods such as "I[5]" training in the service of the possibilities outcomes that interdependent processing yields. The empowering curriculum is ***"The Possibilities Management Paradigm."***

The Processing Team

At Human Technology, Inc., Alex Douds and Dick Pierce were assigned to develop images of organizational teams for the purpose of reorganizing the company. The phenomenon they addressed was thus organizational teaming. Their mode was to become *"one"*—and *growing*—with the phenomenon; in other words, they dedicated their interdependent processing to the phenomenon and, synergistically, to their own growth. Working together as a processing team, they began to think like the organization they were addressing.

Douds and Pierce began by mapping into the phenomenon itself: its functions, components, processes (see Figure 7-3). For their purpose, this meant entering and scaling these dimensions and then interrelating them in a definition of the phenomenal objective:

> *Marketplace functions are discharged by organizational components enabled by human processes.*

The processing team now understood the phenomenal objectives to which they would dedicate their interdependent processing.

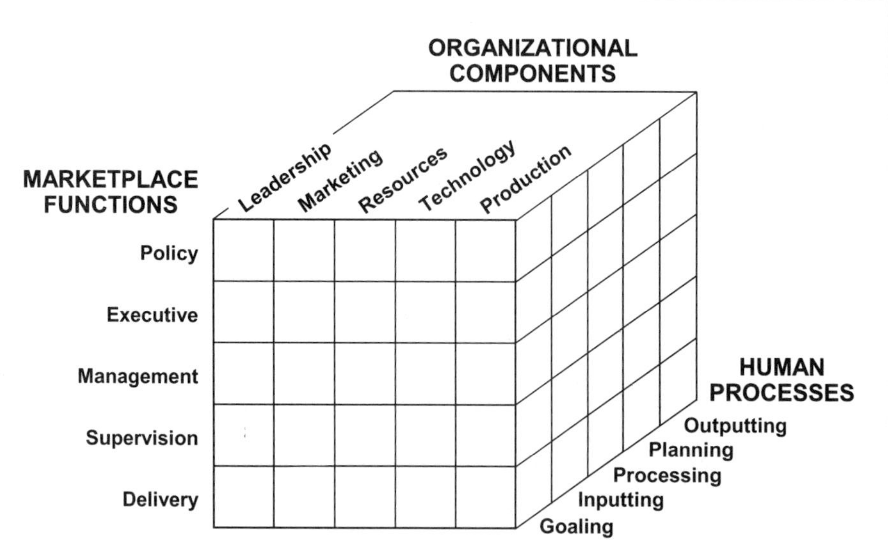

Figure 7-3. Organizational Phenomena

Their organizational experience incomplete, Douds and Pierce next mapped into the marketplace conditions that generate the marketplace functions of the organization (see Figure 7-4). Again, the processing team entered, scaled, and interrelated these dimensions in a phenomenal objective. They discriminated overall marketplace movement from independence and competing to interdependence and collaborating. They labeled this "The Relating Factor," referring in particular to partnered relationships between producers and their customers. Accordingly, they refined their phenomenal objective as follows:

> *Relating marketplace functions are discharged by organizational components enabled by human processes.*

The processing team now understood more accurately the partnering functions of the organizational phenomena.

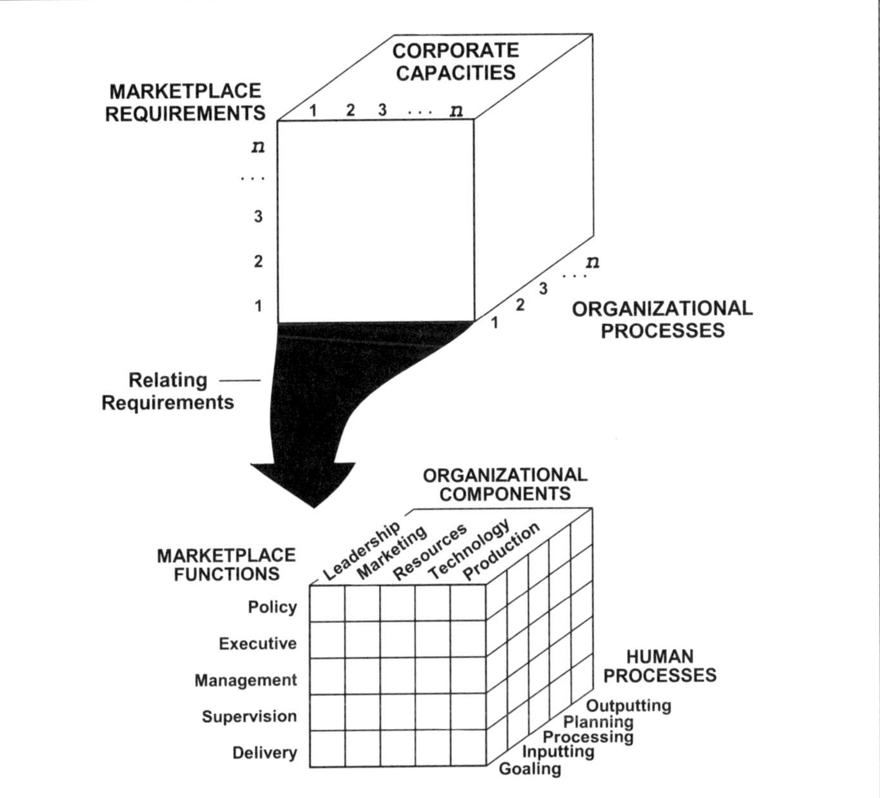

Figure 7-4. Market-Driven Organizational Functions

Finally, to complete their organizational experience, the processing team mapped into the human processes that establish the standards by which we measure the success of organizational teaming (see Figure 7-5). Again, they scaled and interrelated these dimensions in a phenomenal objective. For example, they extended the relating function into human processing teams. They labeled these teams "interdependent processing teams." Accordingly, they redefined the organizational phenomenal objective as follows:

> *Leadership-driven organization functions are discharged by human processing components enabled by information modeling.*

The processing team now had a comprehensive, albeit changing, definition of the organizational phenomenon. This meant they could enter the phenomenon to process interdependently within, between, and among its operations. They could process interdependently with the relating marketing function.

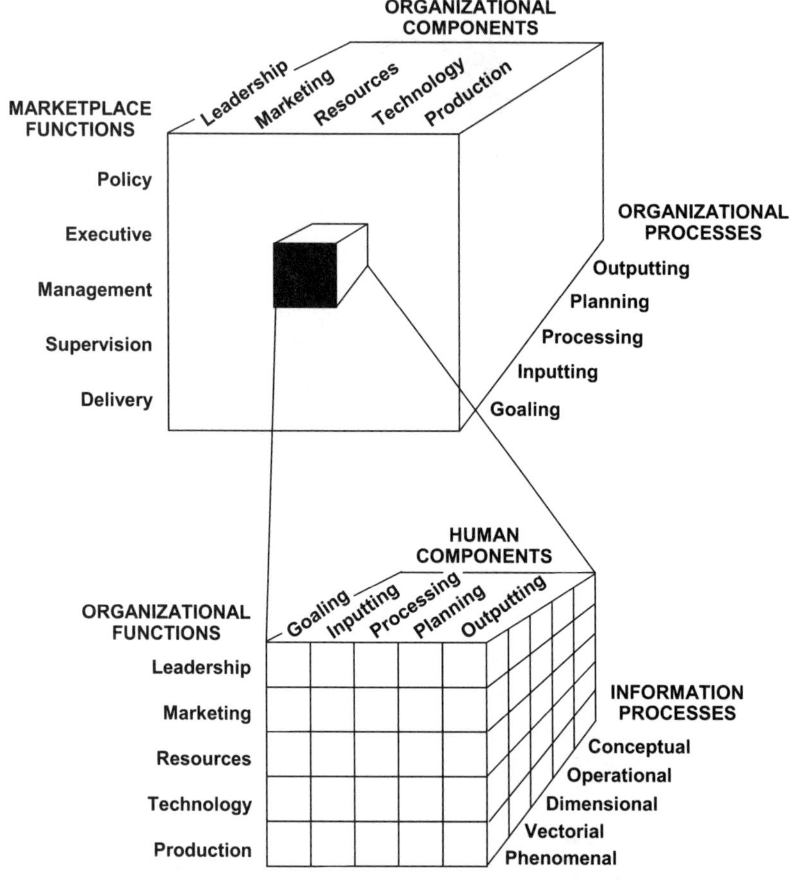

Figure 7-5. Organization-Driven Human Standards

First, the team processed interdependently within the leadership cell shown in Figure 7-6. As may be noted, the policymaking functions are discharged directly by the leadership component enabled by goaling processes.

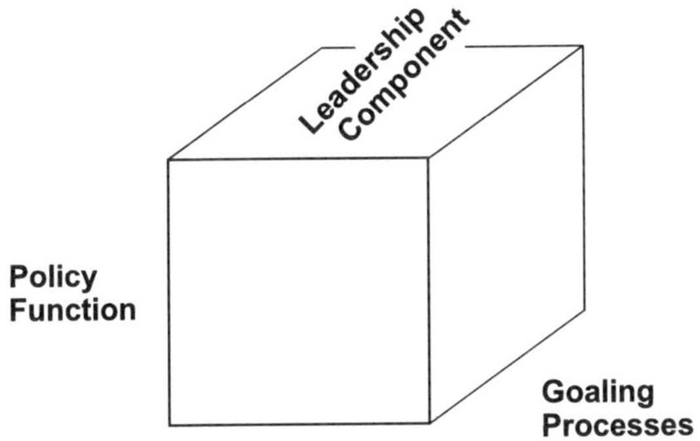

Figure 7-6. Processing Interdependently Within the Leadership Cell

Next, they developed an expanded vision of leadership by processing interdependently within the organizational components: leadership, marketing, resources, technology, production (see Figure 7-7). In addition, the human processes were defined

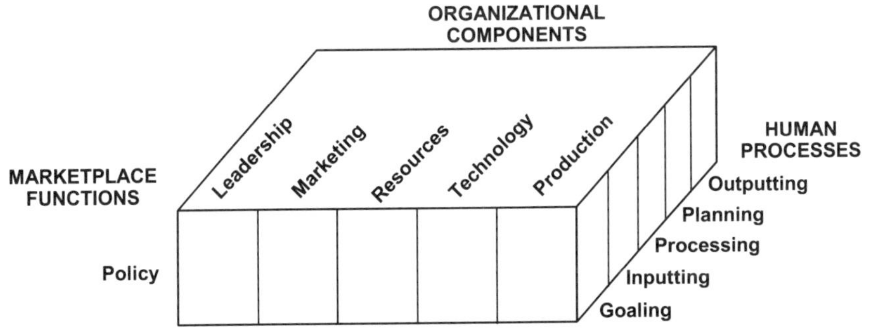

Figure 7-7. Processing Interdependently Between Organizational Components

comprehensively: goaling, inputting, processing, planning, outputting. Policymaking functions were now discharged by all organizational components enabled by comprehensive human processing.

Further, the processing team aligned marketplace functions with leadership-driven components and functions to form a positioning team (see Figure 7-8). With continuous relating to the marketplace, this positioning team had the function of processing interdependently to transform relating functions into marketplace positioning. Douds and Pierce defined the positioning team's phenomenal objective as follows:

> *Relating-positioning functions are discharged by leadership-driven components enabled by comprehensive human processing.*

They labeled this team *"The Possibilities Positioning Team."*

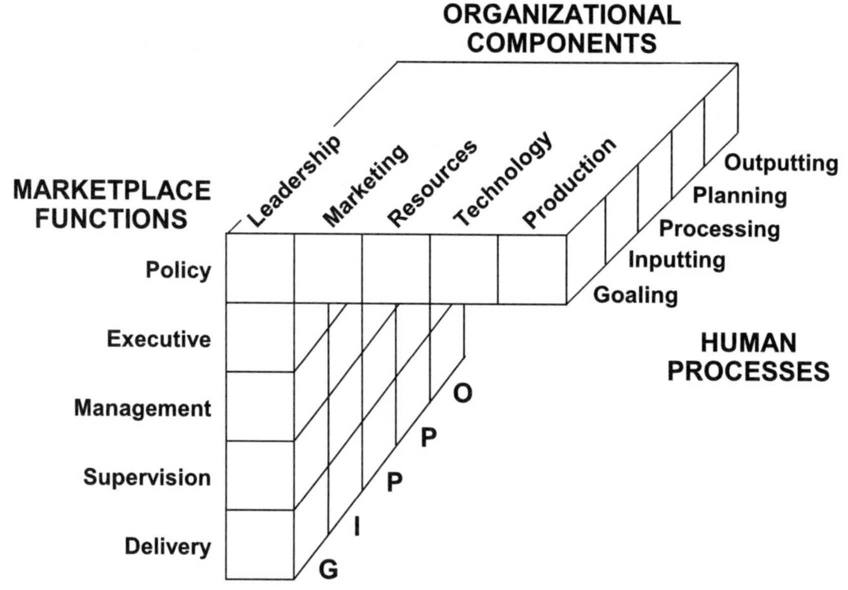

Figure 7-8. Possibilities Positioning Team

Next, the processing team generated and aligned processing teams with this relating-positioning team, as shown in Figure 7-9 (see following page). Here we may note that the teaming systems were represented according to their differential contributions to accomplish the relating positioning:

- *Organizational alignment functions are discharged by market-driven components enabled by interdependent processing teams.*
- *Tailored customer-design and -solution functions are discharged by resource-integration components enabled by interdependent processing teams.*
- *Customized product and service functions are discharged by technology-driven components enabled by interdependent processing teams.*
- *Standardized product functions are discharged by production components enabled by interdependent processing teams.*

Douds and Pierce labeled these organizational teams *"Possibilities Processing Teams."*

In short, the team understood that interdependent processing could occur within, between, and among all operations. For example:

- Within the leadership unit where the policymaking functions are discharged by leadership components enabled by goaling processes;
- Between the policymaking operations where positioning functions are discharged by leadership-driven components enabled by goal-driven processes;
- Among the teaming operations where alignment functions are discharged by market-driven components enabled by goal-driven processes.

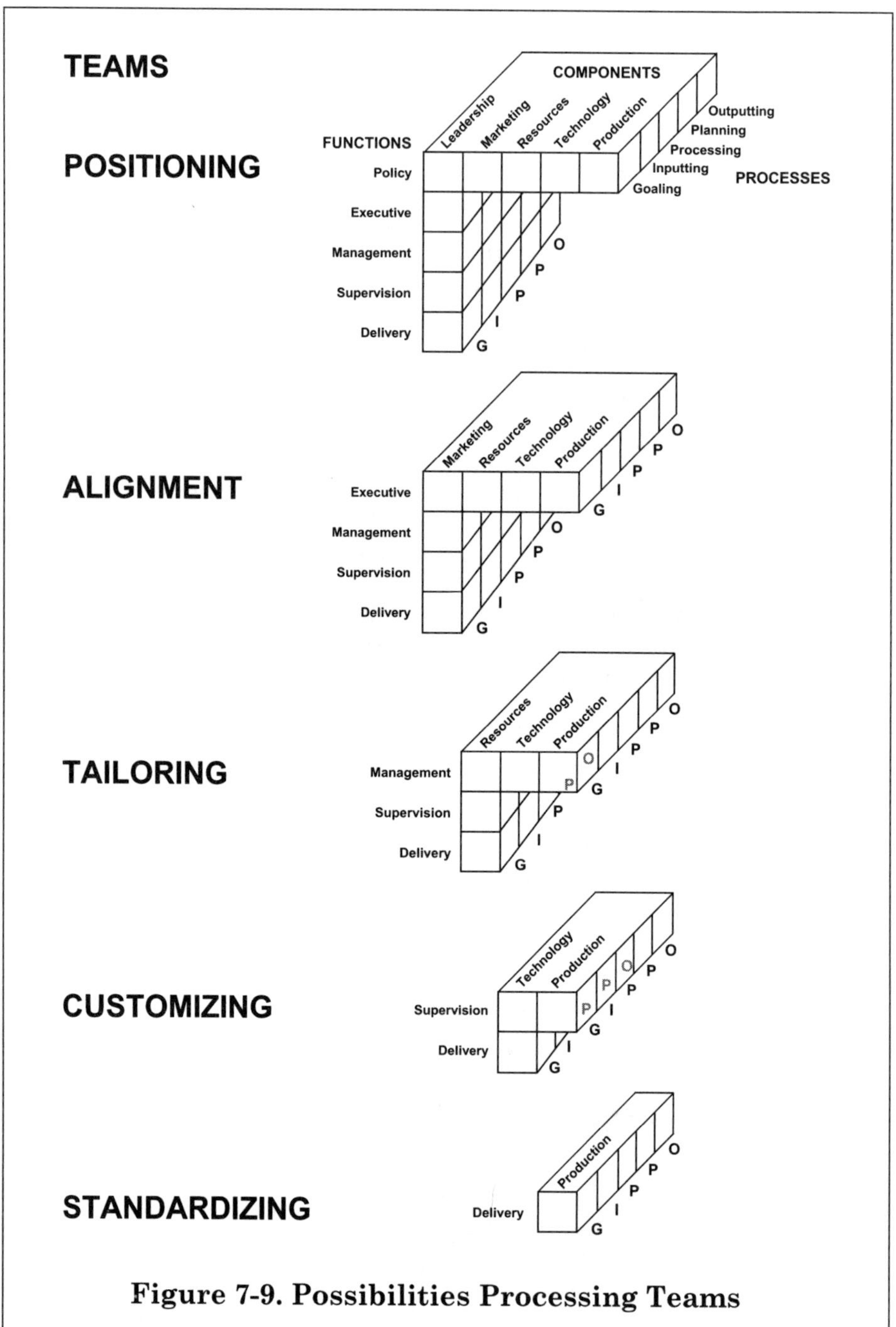

Figure 7-9. Possibilities Processing Teams

Within, between, and among any of these processing teams or units, then, they could apply our I^5 interdependent processing systems to generate continuously changing phenomenal possibilities:

- Processing to generate continuous marketplace positioning;
- Processing to generate continuous organizational alignment;
- Processing to generate continuous customer tailoring;
- Processing to generate continuous product customizing;
- Processing to generate continuous product standardizing.

These organizational processing teams will, themselves, work together synergistically. For instance, as products are standardized, they will enable the organization to reposition itself in the marketplace and, thus, to recycle the organizational processing teams.

The Possibilities Management Paradigm

The possibilities management paradigm applies the possibilities management systems to phenomenal functions. The possibilities management systems emphasize employing interdependent processing systems. We build the "I^5" systems developmentally, or inductively, in training to empower people in generative processing systems.

I^1 *Information relating to define phenomenal operations,*

I^2 *Information representing to image phenomenal dimensions,*

I^3 *Individual processing to generate new phenomenal images,*

I^4 *Interpersonal processing to generate more powerful phenomenal images,*

I^5 *Interdependent processing to generate the most powerful phenomenal images.*

The possibilities management systems may also be employed deductively to innovate when phenomenal functions are already defined: I^5, I^4, I^3, I^2, I^1.

In this context, I^5 is to be taken seriously as "I" to the fifth power. At I^2, the processors' information representations make their ideation exponentially more powerful than at I^1, where the processors have only operational information. Similarly, at I^3, the processors' individual processing makes their ideation exponentially more powerful than at I^2. Likewise, at I^4, the processors' interpersonal processing makes their ideation exponentially more powerful than at I^3. Finally, at I^5, the processors' interdependent processing makes their ideation exponentially more powerful than at I^4. In short, interdependent phenomenal processing is the prepotent mode of generating ideational images of phenomena—any phenomena, all phenomena.

In turn, the phenomenal functions to which we have dedicated our interdependent processing systems include any phenomena. For our purposes, we have emphasized the new capital development system, or organizational phenomena:

MCD *Generating continuous marketplace positioning,*

OCD *Generating continuous organizational alignment,*

HCD *Generating continuous human processing,*

ICD *Generating continuous information building,*

mCD *Generating continuous mechanical tooling.*

The new capital development systems may also be employed inductively, or developmentally: mCD, ICD, HCD, OCD, MCD.

In this context, we must take seriously the definition of the new capital development system: the new sources of capital, or what is *most important* in organizational phenomena.[*] Indeed, the organizational phenomena (OCD) are, themselves, aligned to implement marketplace positioning (MCD). In turn, the human processing phenomena (HCD) are aligned to implement organizational alignment. Similarly, the information-modeling phenomena (ICD) are aligned to become synergistic processing partners with human processing. Finally, the mechanical-tooling phenomena (mCD) are aligned to implement information modeling. The new capital development systems are the prepotent sources of productivity and growth in all organizational systems.

Relatedly, we may view the possibilities management system in its full robustness (see Table 7-1). Here, the I^5 interdependent processing systems constitute the components of the possibilities management systems: I^1, I^2, I^3, I^4, I^5. These I^5 systems may be considered the possibilities leadership systems as well. In turn, the organizational management functions to which they are addressed

---

[*] Carkhuff, R. R., and Berenson, B. G. *The Possibilities Organization.* Amherst, MA: HRD Press, 2000.

are the new capital development systems: MCD, OCD, HCD, ICD, mCD. These NCD systems may be considered the possibilities organization functions as well. Clearly, in deductive processing, the possibilities management/leadership systems may be reversed in order: I^5, I^4, I^3, I^2, I^1. Moreover, the entire matrix may be rotated and the NCD systems dedicated to the growth of possibilities management/leadership systems.

Table 7-1. The Possibilities Management Paradigm

ORGANIZATIONAL MANAGEMENT FUNCTIONS (NCD)	POSSIBILITIES MANAGEMENT SYSTEMS I^1	I^2	I^3	I^4	I^5
MCD	Positioning by I^1	Positioning by I^2	Positioning by I^3	Positioning by I^4	Positioning by I^5
OCD	Aligning by I^1	Aligning by I^2	Aligning by I^3	Aligning by I^4	Aligning by I^5
HCD	Processing by I^1	Processing by I^2	Processing by I^3	Processing by I^4	Processing by I^5
ICD	Modeling by I^1	Modeling by I^2	Modeling by I^3	Modeling by I^4	Modeling by I^5
mCD	Tooling by I^1	Tooling by I^2	Tooling by I^3	Tooling by I^4	Tooling by I^5

In short, the possibilities management paradigm may be defined as managing interdependent processing systems in order to discharge organizational management functions, or, more succinctly, to generate NCD and, in turn, to be generated by NCD.

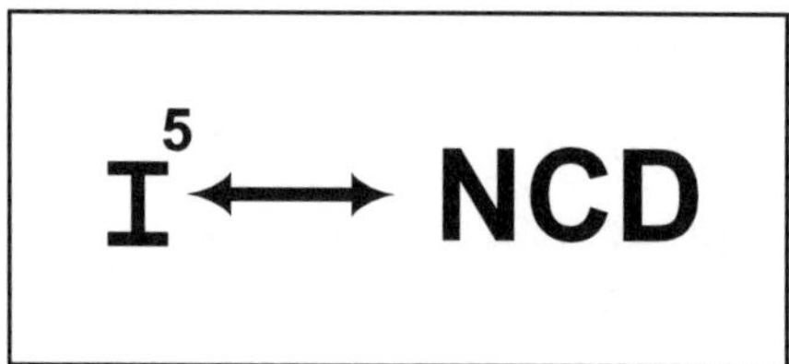

The possibilities management paradigm is a processing map for possibilities leaders: it generates the roads before us; it does so continuously and interdependently; its moving destinations are focused upon NCD.

NCD systems are the spiraling sources of phenomenal growth. "I^5" are the generative processing sources of that growth.

In summary, we have crossed a threshold in civilization. Where once we defined people and organizations by past traditions, possibilities leaders now define them by future requirements. Where once we aspired to independency and competition, possibilities leaders now are dedicated to interdependency and collaboration. The interdependent processing systems are the tools of interdependence and collaboration.

What makes interdependent processing possible is the science of possibilities itself. This new science holds that all phenomena are inherently changeable. Therefore, we can begin to enhance them only by aligning with this changeability. Interdependent processing is the key to actualizing phenomenal experience: relating to the phenomena, representing phenomenal images, generating new and more powerful phenomenal images.

The old science of probabilities holds that the purpose of science is to control phenomena by controlling their variability around some central tendency. To this end, it dedicates its functions:

- Describing phenomenal operations,
- Predicting phenomenal operations,
- Controlling phenomenal operations.

In discharging these functions, the old science is extremely wasteful of the phenomenal information eliminated in so-called *"error variance."* Probabilities leaders forced people and other entities to conform to their static image of our changing potential.

The new science of possibilities holds that all phenomena are continuously changing. To this end, it dedicates its functions:

- Relating to phenomenal operations,
- Empowering phenomenal operations,
- Freeing phenomenal operations.

In discharging these functions, the new science engages us in interdependent processing with changing phenomenal images. Possibilities leaders incorporate and then generate all phenomenal information.

The freeing functions to which the new science is dedicated are defined by response repertoires—in this instance, the repertoires of processing systems. In short, freedom is defined by the phenomenal processing capacities. Possibilities leaders relate to phenomena to merge with their potential. Possibilities leaders empower people and phenomena to actualize new potential. Possibilities leaders free people and phenomena to seek their own differentiated expression. Indeed, the people and other phenomena free themselves when their repertoire of processing systems is sufficient.

In transition, nature's secret is its social nature. Interdependent processing enables us to relate and align with this social nature; to empower and enhance its phenomena; to release or free these phenomena to fulfill their own changeable destinies and, in so doing, to fulfill our own. There is only interdependency and its infinite potential.

POSSIBILITIES MANAGEMENT SYSTEMS

ORGANIZATIONAL MANAGEMENT FUNCTIONS

	I^1 Information Relating Systems	I^2 Information Representing Systems	I^3 Individual Processing Systems	I^4 Interpersonal Processing Systems	I^5 Interdependent Processing Systems
Marketplace Capital Development					
Organizational Capital Development					
Human Capital Development					
Information Capital Development					
Mechanical Capital Development					

THE POSSIBILITIES MANAGEMENT PARADIGM

$\mathbf{I^5} \longleftrightarrow \mathbf{NCD}$

Selected Publications by Authors

The Possibilities Organization. Amherst, MA: HRD Press, 2000.

The New Science of Possibilities. Volumes I & II. Amherst, MA: HRD Press, 2000.

The Possibilities Mind. Amherst, MA: HRD Press, 2000.

Empowering. Amherst, MA: HRD Press, 1990.

The Age of the New Capitalism. Amherst, MA: HRD Press, 1988.

Human Processing and Human Productivity. Amherst, MA: HRD Press, 1986.

The Exemplar. Amherst, MA: HRD Press, 1984.

The Sources of Human Productivity. Amherst, MA: HRD Press, 1983.

Interpersonal Skills and Human Productivity. Amherst, MA: HRD Press, 1982.

Toward Actualizing Human Potential. Amherst, MA: HRD Press, 1981.

The Development of Human Resources. New York, NY: Holt, Rinehart & Winston, 1971.

Helping and Human Relations. Volumes I & II. New York, NY: Holt, Rinehart & Winston, 1969.

Acknowledgments

First, we would like to acknowledge the contributions of the core of research associates in Carkhuff Thinking Systems, Inc., who helped to develop some of the ideas presented in this work:

- Don Benoit, M.A., who contributed operations to information representation,
- Chris Carkhuff, M.A. Cert., who developed the organizational capital models,
- Alvin Cook, Ph.D., who built math models and coding systems,
- Barbara Emmert, Ph.D., who provided information systems perspective,
- Dave Meyers, M.A., who engineered organizational applications,
- Darren Tisdale, M.A., who innovated technological applications.

In addition, we owe a special debt to a number of people—themselves *"possibilities managers"* who made applications of our work at Human Technology, Inc.:

- John Cannon, Ph.D., Vice President, New Capital Development,
- Alex Douds, M.A., Director, Performance Systems Group,
- Sharon Fisher, M.A., Chief Operating Officer,
- Ted W. Friel, Ph.D., Information Technology Consultant,
- Richard Pierce, Ph.D., Director, Organizational Consulting Group.

We are particularly indebted to those scientists who contributed early on to our overall thinking:

- David N. Aspy, D.Ed., Carkhuff Institute,
- George Banks, D.Ed., Carkhuff Institute,
- David H. Berenson, Ph.D., Carkhuff Institute,
- Ralph Bierman, Ph.D., Carkhuff Institute,
- B. R. Bugelski, Ph.D., S.U.N.Y. at Buffalo,
- James Drasgow, Ph.D., S.U.N.Y. at Buffalo,
- Gerald Oliver, M.S., Carkhuff Institute,

- Flora N. Roebuck, D.Ed., Carkhuff Institute,
- Richard Sprinthall, Ph.D., American International College.

We also owe gratitude to pathfinders in business and industry who gave us opportunities to make applications:

- Rick Bellingham, Ph.D., Genzyme, Inc.,
- Russ Campanella, Genzyme, Inc.,
- Dave Champaign, Lotus Corp., IBM,
- Barry Cohen, Ph.D., Parametric Technology Corp.,
- John T. Kelly, M.A., IBM,
- Bill O'Brien, M.A., Parametric Technology Corp.,
- Russ Planitzer, Lazard, Inc.,
- Jack Riley, IBM,
- Peter Rayson, M.Sc., C. Eng., Parametric Technology Corp.,
- Carl Turner, General Electric,
- Norman Turner, General Electric.

We are also indebted to educational advisors with whom we processed interdependently to make extensive applications:

- Cheryl Aspy, D.Ed., University of Oklahoma,
- William Anthony, Ph.D., Boston University,
- Karen Banks, D.Ed., James Madison University,
- Sally Berenson, D.Ed., North Carolina State University,
- Terry Bergeson, Ph.D., Superintendent of Public Instruction, Washington,
- Mikal Cohen, Ph.D., Boston University,
- Andrew H. Griffin, D.Ed., Assistant Superintendent of Public Instruction, Washington,
- Shirley McCune, D.S.W., Director, Multi-States LINKS Project, Washington,
- Jeannette Tamagini, Ph.D., Rhode Island College.

Also, we express our gratitude to the trainers of Human Capital Development at the HRD Center, American International College, for piloting some of our work:

- Debbie Decker Anderson, D.Ed., Director,
- Cindy Littlefield, M.A., Associate Director,
- Susan Mackler, M.A., Holyoke Community College,
- Richard Muise, M.A., Assistant Director.

There are those who deserve our appreciation for their support in transforming these early manuscripts into readable books:

- Dave Burleigh, D B Associates for Marketing,
- Bob Carkhuff, HRD Press, for positioning,
- John Cannon, Ph.D., Human Technology, Inc., for his critical readings,
- Mary George, M.A., HRD Press, for editing.

Jean Miller deserves an exceptional note of recognition for implementing our *"rapid prototyping"* method of writing: about one dozen versions of each book were produced before final copy. Not only did she turn around high-quality typing, she also turned around high quality with timeliness. Not only did she generate creative graphics and layout, she also continuously retrieved lost files and, on at least two occasions, tracked down misdelivered manuscripts. These books are as much her books as ours!

Finally, we owe a debt of everlasting love and gratitude to those people who have been absolute in their commitment to enabling us to actualize our vision: our wives, Bernice and Gloria, who related to our experience, empowered our potential, and released us to the freedom of our scientific pursuits. For nearly 50 years, we have been saying, *"Give us another year and we'll get there."* Well, the *year* is up! And we got there!